Permaculture

A Spiritual Approach

Craig Gibsone & Jan Martin Bang

𝑓 FINDHORN PRESS

Permaculture

A Spiritual Approach

Craig Gibsone & Jan Martin Bang

f FINDHORN PRESS

© Craig Gibsone & Jan Martin Bang, 2015

The right of Craig Gibsone & Jan Martin Bang to be identified as
the authors of this work has been asserted by them in accordance
with the Copyright, Designs and Patents Act 1998.

Published in 2015 by Findhorn Press, Scotland

ISBN 978-1-84409-657-2

A CIP record for this title is available from the British Library.

Edited by Michael Hawkins
Cover design by Thierry Bogliolo
Cover photos by Michael Mitton
Interior illustrations: see page 171.
Interior design by Damian Keenan
Printed and bound in the EU

Published by
Findhorn Press
117-121 High Street,
Forres IV36 1AB,
Scotland, UK

t +44 (0)1309 690582
f +44 (0)131 777 2711
e info@findhornpress.com
www.findhornpress.com

Contents

Acknowledgements

This has been a collaborative work by the two of us over a period of nearly two years, so the first thing we want to say is thank you to each other for a cooperative effort which has forged a deep friendship between us.

We have been helped along the way by a large number of people. Of course the danger with naming them is that someone may be left out. We take that risk and apologize to anyone who feels left out. We want to thank Graham Bell, Helene Bøhler, Roger Doudna, Siobhan Dyson, Alan Watson Featherstone, Dorothy Maclean, Gilad Margalit, Lyndall Parry, John Talbott and Alex Walker for your various contributions to this book.

A special thanks must go to Sabine Weeke and the staff at Findhorn Press, who have coped so patiently with all our delays and our chaos. Without you this project would never have seen the light of day.

Most of all, we would like to thank the thousands of people we have had contact with through seminars and courses over the last decades, who have helped to shape our own ideas. They have been open to the spiritual, or invisible dimension that we have discovered within, through and by Permaculture.

It is this social interplay that gives Permaculture and Ecovillage Design its direction and momentum. We are both grateful to be part of this living, developing tradition.

Jan Martin Bang & Craig Gibsone

Authors' Introduction

From its beginning Permaculture has defined an Ethic that we are using here in this book; People Care, Earth Care and Fair Share. This automatically implies that Permaculture has a dimension beyond the merely material, measurable or technical.

Ethics relates to moral philosophy and borders on that inner space we find in each of us, that some might refer to as spiritual. This has nothing to do directly with any specific religion, but suggests that there is a hidden dimension within each of us that we need to take into account when designing for human beings.

There has been a debate for many years within Permaculture between those who want to keep the subject strictly materialistic, and those who want to include spiritual dimensions. We have followed this debate and our aim is to keep it open and productive.

The new scientific paradigm, opened up by cutting edge research in quantum physics, indicates that the universe is not only material but that there are other dimensions. These are still largely unexplored by science but ignoring these is profoundly unscientific. Curiosity about the cosmos that we live in would hopefully invite us to explore further.

The vast majority of people and cultures on this planet recognize another dimension, something that resembles the spiritual. This is true both in time and space. Archaeology reveals that way back in the so-called Stone Age we were celebrating rituals that indicate a belief in powers and dimensions that can only be described as spiritual.

Travelling around the world today, we find that most cultures, especially the more traditional ones, acknowledge the same thing. Indeed, learning from aboriginal peoples would be extremely difficult, if not completely pointless, without understanding and accepting their view of the hidden forces within themselves and their environment.

In order for Permaculture to be truly holistic and truly speak to all people and to all cultures, we need to recognize this dimension that we call the spiritual. This does not mean that we need to become practising Catholics, Muslims or Shamans, or that we need to preach any specific religion in our courses. But we do need to create a dialogue, we need to understand, and be understood. To imply that this spiritual dimension does not exist would be to deny ourselves perhaps the most meaningful exchange between us.

We truly believe that Permaculture has to address this in a positive way.

This book is a contribution to this widening of Permaculture. We are offering this not as a provocation to the debate which sometimes has assumed the form of an argument, even a conflict, but as a reaching out and an invitation to a dialogue.

Craig Gibsone and Jan Martin Bang,
April 2015

CHAPTER ONE

Permaculture, Spirituality and the New Paradigm

There is a perfect pattern and plan running through the whole of life, and you are part of that perfect pattern and plan.

— *EILEEN CADDY*

A classic definition of Permaculture is that it is a set of design tools, based on models from natural ecologies, that we use as templates for designing the infrastructure we need to create a sustainable future. This is a good working definition, emphasizing that it's a way of thinking, that we use natural models, and that we can design anything we need using these models.

We like to add that Permaculture is a dialogue with nature at a time when we have stopped listening, that it is a series of questions leading us into the future, so it's not dogmatic, but adapts to the circumstances of the situation.

In addition, Permaculture is a social organism, with members in many countries throughout the world. We have a strong and vibrant communication system at local level, at regional level, and with occasional international convergences.

Permaculture is also about taking the responsibility to act locally, where you are, when you can, with the resources available to you in that place. We may rail at distant miscarriages of justice, but if we can't do very much about them, we may well be better off using our energy doing something about our local situation. That old well-worn phrase, *"Think globally, act locally"* sits very well with Permaculture.

Permaculture and Findhorn

In the 1960s, while the founders of Permaculture were exploring the idea of a sustainable culture, the founders of Findhorn were beginning to explore the dimensions of spiritual community and co-creation with nature.

Both were drawing upon the wisdom inherent in nature, whether the strength of connections in a rain forest or the etheric patterns over-lighting the natural worlds.

The life force of this living planet was acknowledged to be working with the spirit of nature and with the nature spirits, both finding a resonance in the diverse cultural expressions exploding in the '60s, spiritual in the case of Findhorn, as well as environmental where Permaculture had a stronger focus. It would take until the 1990s before we saw a respect for one another growing and that there was strength in supporting one another and sharing our perspectives.

Bill Mollison

David Holmgren

The founders of both Findhorn and Permaculture drew upon the wisdom of cultures that had sustained themselves for thousands of years, taking their best practices and adapting them to the present day. In particular reintroducing the cultural relationship of agriculture that is celebrated by local communities and linked to the seasons and cycles of nature and its abundance, diversity and beauty. This last aspect grew fast as modern farming became more an agro-business model of inputs and outputs exhausting the soils, destroying all those other communities of life that enhance and create resilience.

In the book *Permaculture 1,* published in 1978, Bill Mollison and David Holmgren wrote:

> *"We do not believe that a society can survive if it lacks values, direction, and ethics, and thus relinquishes control over its future destiny."*

This was the first book to describe Permaculture and right from the start the founders had brought in the invisible qualities of values and ethics, so close to spirituality.

Ten years later Mollison published the *Designer's Manual,* generally accepted amongst Permaculturalists to be the defining book on the subject. Here is a whole section devoted to ethics. Mollison introduces this by describing how they researched older religious and cooperative groups, looking for general principles.

This is what they formulated as the Permaculture ethic:

1. **CARE OF THE EARTH:**
   Provision for all life systems to continue and multiply.

2. **CARE OF PEOPLE:**
   Provision for people to access those resources necessary for their existence.

3. **SETTING LIMITS TO POPULATION AND CONSUMPTION:**
   By governing our own needs, we can set resources aside to further the above principles.

With a little tweak on the last one, calling it Fair Share, this ethic forms the framework for our book on the spiritual aspects of Permaculture.

In this *Designer's Manual* Mollison goes on to write that he has developed a personal philosophy close to Taoism, defining this as working with rather than against nature.

It's the question that is most important, that is what defines the answer we are looking for, and he gives as an example two questions. In one we ask ourselves, "What can I get from this land?" In the other, "What does this land have to give if I cooperate with it?"

The New Paradigm

Our modern scientific thinking is largely based upon the change in thinking that occurred around the time of Descartes, 1596 to 1650. Until then all things had been connected in some way, the world view being based upon the foundations laid down by the Greek philosophers two thousand years earlier.

Descartes separated mind and matter, believing that a complete understanding of the laws of mathematics would unlock the knowledge of the universe. This created a new way of looking at the world, and a number of thinkers followed Descartes, building a paradigm of the world completely different from how the universe was understood earlier.

Francis Bacon, 1561 to 1626, saw the aim of science being not just an understanding of the universe, but also a means of controlling it. Galileo Galilei, 1564 to 1642, maintained that matter had to be studied only by quantifying it. If it can't be measured it has no meaning and by implication doesn't exist.

Building upon these philosophers, Isaac Newton, 1642 to 1726, showed how the universe worked as a great mechanism, and formulated some of the laws that govern this mechanism such as gravity, mass and motion.

These must have been exciting times, building a new view of the world. But, as in many breakthroughs in science and in thinking, it was just another way of looking at the world, not THE ONLY WAY.

There are two defining features of this world view, which gives it the name "the Materialist Reductionist Paradigm". It was only concerned with the things that can be seen and measured, and it took these apart in order to study them. It was exactly this last approach that led to new ways of seeing things a few hundred years later. The hard science that started with Descartes and which was developed by Newton finally led to amazing discoveries as physicists cracked open the atom at the beginning of the twentieth century.

A number of scientists, including Niels Bohr, Albert Einstein, Werner Heisenberg, Wolfgang Pauli, Max Planck and Erwin Schrödinger worked together to explore the frontiers of science. What they found was not easy for them to accept. The new concepts of time, matter, space, cause and effect did not always conform to the scientific world in which they had been brought up.

In Fritjof Capra's book, *The Turning Point* he quotes Heisenberg:

> *"The violent reaction to the recent development of modern physics can only be understood when one realises that here the foundations of physics have started moving."*

The terms that might be applied to this new world include organic, holistic and ecological. These scientists were looking for a systems view, a general systems theory. Through their work they realized that our long tradition of mystical thought, begun by Shamans and kept alive by the established world religions, echo the ideas that were coming to the forefront in the new physics. Cutting edge science was beginning to open a fruitful dialogue with spirituality and religion.

It's often the case that with older, spiritual traditions, the way things are formulated may sound quite outrageous to us today, especially if we are still deeply embedded in the old materialist reductionist paradigm. However, communing with the spirit of the mountain may actually not be so very far away from appreciating the energy of the mountain.

❧✺❧

Gradually these new ways of looking at the world seeped through into the western world. Arthur Koestler wrote in *The Yogi and the Commissar*, published in 1945:

"After all it is only three centuries since God became a mathematician and we have plenty of time before us for other transformations. The monopoly of quantitative measurements is drawing to its close, but already new principles of explanation begin to emerge."

Kees Zoeteman writing in *Gaia – Sophia* commented that: "In nuclear physics, the Cartesian distinction between mind and matter, the observer and the observed, could no longer be made."

The qualities of matter composed of atoms depend upon the way we observe this matter, what type of equipment we use and which of our senses we bring into play. Matter doesn't really exist at all, but shows "tendencies to exist". The clear distinction between observer and the observed was no longer seen to be objective, but subjective. Mass and energy became interchangeable. They were manifestations of space and time that appeared differently according to how they were observed.

A serious change occurred here in the history of science, and in the way we perceive the world around us. In the old paradigm all reality was seen to be material or physical. Rupert Sheldrake in his book *The Science Delusion* described this paradigm:

"There is no reality but material reality. Matter is unconscious. Evolution is purposeless."

This view of the world permeated every level of thinking and influenced the way society in the western world was structured and came to spread throughout the world as a consequence of the colonial expansion.

Bede Griffiths writes that: "Over a period of nearly three centuries in the West the philosophy of materialism has come to permeate every level of society."

We really enjoy Rudolf Steiner's wry description of the old paradigm that he expressed in 1924:

"Nature is a unity, with forces interacting from all sides. Those whose eyes are open to these forces will understand nature. But what does today's science do? It takes a little glass plate and puts a carefully prepared something-or-other on it, gets rid of everything else and peers at it through something called a microscope. That is the very opposite of what we ought to be doing if we want to comprehend the full dimensions of the world."

The new physics created a foundation from which we could start replacing the mechanical model of the universe with an organic model. In this new view we perceive a return to traditional wisdom and spirituality. In the old materialist reductionist worldview, science and religion were often seen as competing spheres. This polarization is now increasingly felt as hindering our way forward in discovering what the world is and how it operates. This is perhaps one of the basic, key qualities to the new paradigm, and one that Permaculture needs to take into itself.

John Wilkes comments that:

> *"As long as we continue to consider nature, organisms and life as something merely physical, technological and chemical we are missing a comprehension of the whole picture. There are obviously much more subtle aspects which nature is trying to show us, if only we are willing to see."*

In many ways it's like the transition from black and white to colour. Sure, we can get a long way with the old black and white drawings and photographs, and in some circumstances b/w is actually preferable. But try to explain to someone who has no colour vision what colours are like, and you may find yourself up against an insurmountable barrier.

How to describe the difference between red and green? What could it possibly mean, to see red? Can only black men sing the blues? To someone incapable of seeing colours, these kinds of statements may have no meaning.

Sir Arthur Eddington, the British astrophysicist who lived from 1882 to 1944, wrote:

> *"The stuff of the world is mind-stuff."*

His colleague Sir James Jeans wrote:

> *"The universe begins to look more like a great thought than like a great machine. Mind no longer appears as an accidental intruder into the realm of matter; we are beginning to suspect that we ought rather to hail it as the creator and governor of the realm of matter."*

This does not necessarily mean that the old paradigm was wrong. Clearly it's a very good way of creating a framework for mechanical engineering, it's a good way of doing technical work with water, electricity and other substances. We might see conventional science as the tip of an iceberg. There is still much to be discovered, and different scientific approaches represent different, complementary views of the world.

Let us be open-minded and flexible in our seeking as we dive deeper into the hidden layers of the iceberg. To deny their existence is profoundly unscientific.

Thoughts become realities when they form the basis for action. Thoughts, desires and ambitions have shaped the modern world: the technologies, the social systems, and the economy. If our technologies are polluting, our social systems unable to care for everyone, and our economics fail to distribute food and services to all people, it must be that the thoughts that underpin these systems are to blame. We need new thoughts.

Looking at how life has evolved it seems that confronted by difficult situations, life has taken unexpected directions in order to overcome them. Being forced into a new way of thinking may be the most important aspect of the crisis that we find ourselves in. The only way out and through is by changing the way we relate to the world. Today we need this new paradigm more than ever.

Several of the new scientists have described the universe as a "Great Thought", an image that can be used as a tool for expanding our own thinking. We need to be brave enough to try thinking thoughts that seem alien to us in order to explore the new paradigm. Today it's actually a scientific handicap if you are not prepared to entertain new ideas, but prefer to stay stuck in a familiar world that you feel comfortable with.

In one course that we taught the idea that water may have memory was mentioned, and encountered stiff resistance from a couple of the more academically minded participants, despite the fact that the very property of water being able to hold information is being scientifically researched at the present time. Instead of welcoming new unfamiliar ways of thinking as a gateway to new discoveries, they retreated into old dogmatic ways of thinking that dismissed new ideas as rubbish.

When we do this, we close the portal of discovery.

In our world today we are experiencing a multiple existential crisis, with seemingly intractable economic, environmental and social problems of such dimensions that solutions are hard to find. What is usually offered as a solution is a series of technological fixes, all based on the same thinking that pervades the old materialist reductionist paradigm.

Of course, good design and intelligent planning are really important, but we need something more than that. Even to offer Permaculture solutions based on the old hard technical fix will not help. We need a new way of thinking, a new relationship to ourselves and to the planet.

What insights might I get from thinking about the universe as a thought? How might I relate to all animals, plants and rocks in the landscape as full of intelligence and ideas? If those landscape elements and I could form a "task force" together, how might we transform this landscape into a creative, abundant and fertile ecology? What is nature trying to say to me? Can we enter into a dialogue?

David Spangler, spiritual teacher and author, manages to sum this up eloquently:

> *"If there's one leap our consciousness has to make – and it's a quantum leap – it's how to be able to function, embody, look at and deal with multiple views of reality simultaneously and to be comfortable with that and not insist that reality only follows one particular course."*

Observation

One of the basic ideas in Permaculture is observation. It's the first thing we need to do in order to get a design going. If it's a garden or a smallholding we ought to observe for at least a year, see the seasons come and go and how they interact. If it's a business we need to check out the market, the suppliers and the raw materials. If it's an educational course we are designing we have to know who the group is, what their needs are and what are the aims of the course.

Johann Wolfgang von Goethe, 1749 to 1832, developed a comprehensive exercise in observation that we use in many Permaculture courses.

First of all we can describe the thing itself that we are observing, be it a plant, a guild of plants, a farm or a large scale ecology. This is pretty straightforward; size, shape, and colour are all easily identifiable characteristics.

The next step is to look at the context of the object. If it's a tree, what are the companion plants, animals and insects? What is the geology, the microclimate? If it's a larger phenomenon, an Ecovillage for instance, what is the social and political context? What about the larger geographical and climatic context?

A third step is to look at the life cycle. If it's a plant, it will probably have a life cycle of seed – sprout – leaves – flower – fruit – seed. Where in this cycle is the plant we are observing? Whole ecologies have life cycles, and often come to a mature, steady state of equilibrium. Is the ecology we are observing in a pioneer stage, maybe? Human groups and communities also go through a life cycle of youth, maturity and old age. For example, The Findhorn Community, after over 50 years of steady growth, will be quite different from the Findhorn of 40 years ago.

Lastly we might look at how this object feels to us, how we are affected emotionally, in our feelings. Can we find some symbol to represent it to us? Can we sum it up? Does it have connotations of other things familiar to us?

By going through these questions we build up a comprehensive picture of the object in its setting that includes us, the observer, our feelings and our thoughts about the object and create an holistic view.

Our own state of consciousness and connectedness with the whole determines what kind of actions we take. The consequences of our actions will create a certain kind of world. Now we can begin to see the relationship between the spirit and the physical and its function within Permaculture. We can start to see that all things play an intrinsic role in the web of life.

It becomes evident that the relationships between humans, plants, animals, infrastructure, earth, air, fire, and water connect to the spirit; the seen and the unseen. The connectedness of the whole expands out into the infinite universe.

When observing the world around us, and the events within it, we need to remove our prejudices and interpretations.

One of the exercises we often do in a Permaculture Design Course is to take time to go into nature, asking each participant to find a spot where they feel comfortable alone, and sit there for at least 30 minutes in silence. They are given the opportunity to share any insights in a group conversation afterwards.

We are often under the impression that observation is done with our physical senses, our eyes, ears, nose and mouth. As complete human beings we also have feelings, intuitions, emotions and thoughts, and these are additional sensing tools that we can use for observation. What feelings and thoughts does the observed phenomena arouse in us? We may find a connection to the thing, it may become a part of us, or our observations make us a part of it.

We have seen that this is something that modern science has confirmed. The observer becomes part of the observed object. *All things are interconnected in a great web of life.* If we are going to use "deep observation" we need to take into account all of our responses, our feelings, emotions and intuitions.

Our experience of these deep observation exercises in our courses reveals that the majority of participants appreciate qualities that go far beyond the merely physical.

These ideas we use actively in the Permaculture courses that we lead. The second of Mollison's questions: "What does this land have to give if I cooperate with it?" implies that the landscape has a direction, an intelligence, even a will of its own. Here we are not so far from the old Shamans who were in contact with Nature Spirits. Biodynamic farmers and gardeners also cooperate with what they call Elemental Beings, and at Findhorn we work with the Devas.

We have seen that the starting point of all Permaculture design is observation. When looking at design for our own inner garden or state of consciousness, inner and outer observation plays an important role. The ancient Celts revered the spirits of the four elements Earth, Air, Fire and Water that they believed combined to manifest all creation. Through observation of these four elements they obtained insight into the rhythms of nature and understood them to also be the rhythms of their own lives.

Through these observations they learnt to "work with nature and not against" and discovered the connection between the natural world and our own human nature. Witchcraft in ancient history was known as "The Craft of the Wise" because those that followed that path were in tune with the forces of nature, had knowledge of herbs and medicines, gave "council" and were valuable parts of the village and community as Shamanic healers and leaders.

They understood that mankind is not superior to nature, the Earth and its creatures but instead we are simply one of the many parts, both seen and unseen, that combine to make the whole.

These wise people understood that what we take or use, we must return in kind to maintain balance and equilibrium. In their ancient spiritual practices they were already anticipating the three Permaculture ethics. A further example of this is seen in the teachings of Jesus where he tells us to contemplate (observe) the flowers and learn from them how to live. The Buddha also is said to have given a "silent sermon" once during which he held up a flower and gazed at it. After a while, a monk called Mahakasyapa, began to smile. He is said to have been the only one who had understood the sermon.

According to legend, that smile (that is to say realization) was handed down by twenty-eight successive masters and much later became the origin of Zen.

Permaculture and Nature

We look for and support the natural strength within systems, seeing the relationships between the earth and the air, the fire and the water. Seeing the whole as one interconnecting web of life. Spending time alone in the landscape, we can observe throughout the year the way the sun shines upon the land, creating the seasons and cycles, and drawing forth abundance.

We observe how the rain falls upon the land, and how the flow of the water affects soils, creating places of fertility and microclimates, and where it can be best retained and so creating even more diversity. We observe also the wind and its directions, as it sculpts the vegetation, massaging the landscape, creating places of shelter and exposure. As we walk the landscape we sense the earth beneath us, and its places of natural fertility.

There is a great danger in our time of the emerging Anthropocene; that our species could witness its own self-annihilation along with all of our creativity, knowledge and wisdom, consumed by greed and selfishness. But there is also the possibility that the Anthropocene will be a time of conscious co-creation, that the fecundity of this planet will continue to amaze and enthral, that we can write our story in the fossils of the future as one of incredible self awareness.

We need our worldviews to merge, to strengthen and support one another and all communities of life: Permaculture and spirituality are totally compatible. Some of us work with the spirit of nature, while others work with the nature spirits. Both are coming from that place of co-creation, working with nature.

In Findhorn, we work with the principle "co-creation with nature". Through this partnering with nature, the Earth and all its living creatures, a deepening of the connection with the whole occurs. Dorothy Maclean, one of the three founders of Findhorn, worked with guidance from the nature spirits (Devas) when it came to interaction with the Earth and its plants and animals; a direct link with the spirit world. Eileen Caddy worked with guidance from God, while Peter Caddy carried out this guidance in faith and love.

The Findhorn Foundation community became a physical manifestation of a pure connection into the spirit world, through love and faith, and through this self-less connection with the infinite life force a graceful dance took place between the physical and spiritual realms. As we begin to explore the relationship between these seemingly different paradigms, we see co-creation arising.

Before the materialist reductionist paradigm it seems that all cultures contained defining spiritual beliefs. It may be that Permaculture is essentially materialist and scientific, a set of design tools to be used for designing "things". However, it would be limiting to expect Permaculture to ignore an aspect and a quality that has permeated human life since the beginning of our existence as a species, and which has been suspended for only a few hundred years by a very small segment of humanity.

Indeed, the very success of the materialist reductionist paradigm has led us to the brink of environmental, economic and social breakdown. Could a shift to re-include spirituality in our culture help us to regain our equilibrium? We have already seen that the breakthroughs in quantum physics echoed some of the insights of ancient and modern mystics and sages, confirming that all is one, that matter is an illusion, "as above, so below".

Many thinkers and writers are suggesting that the most progressive aspects of science are moving towards a union with the universal aspects of spiritual belief.

David Holmgren, the co-founder of Permaculture asks:

"Can we really imagine a sustainable world without a spiritual life in some form?"

Design

Permaculture moves from observing the world, to finding patterns in nature, and using these to design the sustainable world of the future. We also use Permaculture to design our lives, not only the "things" that surround us. Your life would clearly be better if it was integrated into the already existing life design of the planet.

In this way, you might design your life to go with the flow of nature, the nature of one's self, and the nature of life surrounding you. There is a beauty, a joy, and an abundance in nature and we sense its spirit. It feeds our body and soul, we are one or even more. The dance of life continues to become even more beautiful, joyful and abundant.

One of the qualities we perceive in nature is an ever ascending attempt to increase complexity. More complex ecologies take longer to evolve, but attain a greater resilience, are more sustainable. Consciousness is the highest form of complexity and holds integration and differentiation together.

Spirituality and Permaculture in Findhorn

The Findhorn Foundation Community is probably one of the best demonstrations of a full-featured Permaculture human settlement.

In Findhorn we work closely with the three Permaculture ethics and as a spiritual community many of our activities such as sacred dance, group sharing and other social activities provide an opportunity for self expression and fellowship.

Many programmes offer activities such as group discovery games, again as an opportunity to express and connect as a group. Within the daily rhythm of work, of morning and afternoon meditations an attunement process is adopted within the working departments and programmes as an opportunity to find stillness, grounding and to connect with spirit. In the words of Eileen Caddy:

"both eyes on heaven and both feet on the earth".

These activities all play an important role within the people care ethic. Spirituality also involves some form of self-reflection by observing what is arising within you, sensing your place in the vast space of existence and observing its cycles. Also your response to the pressures of life: it could be a difficult person or a weed in your garden.

First and foremost of the Permaculture ethics is EARTHCARE, co-creating with nature. Here at Findhorn one of our best examples is Trees for Life, a

Scottish conservation charity dedicated to the regeneration and restoration of the Caledonian Forest in the Highlands of Scotland; a vision of Scotland once again reforested and full of life. There is a longer description of Trees for Life in Chapter 3.

Earthcare is about ecological and sustainable settlements and gardens, using resources wisely and valuing the earth, the air, the water and the sun, from which we extract our needs, and thinking about future generations and what we bequeath them.

PEOPLECARE is one of the most well-practiced disciplines for how we govern and dissolve power, using the group building techniques from "Process Oriented Psychology" (POP), group discovery activities, Game of Transformation, deep democracy, through to meditation, incarnational spirituality, appreciative enquiry, non-violent communication, singing and dancing, work departments,, sanctuary, festivals, etc. The success of the community can be attributed to the attention given to the individual and their place in the collective. Group building processes are like compost continually enriching the soil and feeding one's whole being

Then there is FAIRSHARE. Within the Findhorn Foundation there is a strong sense of service where we share, share, share and share again. From cooking, cleaning, maintenance, home care, finance, management, and cleaning after our community meals. There are dozens of Community-owned buildings: houses, the Community Centre, meditation spaces, workshop venues and large beautiful gardens.

Our carpooling system, the Moray Carshare, currently has over 50 members and we share nine cars amongst us. The cars are placed at three different locations in and around Findhorn and Forres. The carpool is run in a democratic way, like a community interest company, using a methodology called Sociocracy.

The NFA (New Findhorn Association) is our wider community-shared way of living; it is an association of individual members and organizations who subscribe to a set of core values. The main purpose for the NFA is to serve as an umbrella organization and to facilitate and encourage development of the community.

We share our Windfarms to provide our energy; our local hinterland association cares for local dune landscape and pine plantation, with the wood co-operative harvesting firewood, and food production from the community owned Cullerne Gardens.

The community has established a community bank, called Ekopia Resource Exchange. This permits the community to raise share issues for specific projects within the community.

We know of no other community that is as large and full-featured as we are, stretching from the Isle of Erraid to the Highlands of Scotland and the Bioregion of Moray, whilst embracing the ethics and the principles of Permaculture and spirituality.

•

From The Bush to The Findhorn Garden

I HAD THE FORTUNATE EXPERIENCE of being born in the bush on a small farm in Australia. Barefoot and without electricity, all of our domestic water was captured in the wet season for the rest of the year.

My mother would take me with her to milk the cow, feed the chickens, wash the clothes by hand, split firewood, harvest fruit and veggies and when old enough, kill, pluck and gut chickens, finally giving me the gun to hunt wild birds and animals all for the table.

Spending many hours in the kitchen cooking on a wood stove, she would sit me on the kitchen table while she cooked, baked and preserved food, and then used the treadle sewing machine. We also collected wild flowers to make still-life arrangements for her to paint while I doodled.

The hardest of all was washing the sheets out in the laundry, keeping the wood fired copper boiler going while stirring the sheets with a big wooden pole. She and all the farmers' wives were supported by the Country Women's Association (CWA).

It was full of permaculture Ethics, Attitudes and Principles: not stated, just simply lived.

Then with my father it was quite a different story, being involved in clearing the land of its indigenous forests, animals and people, and then turning it into irrigated pastureland for cows. We felled trees, built stockyards, barns, hay sheds, fences, and dug irrigation ditches, all by hand. He had a magic white powder that he gave me to sprinkle round all the ant's nests and throughout the vegetable patch and orchards. It was called DDT.

He showed me maps and charts, taking me on field trips to the distant hills, visiting dams with drowned forests poking through them where our irrigation water came from, and on the way home we would go by deserted farms and orchards to scavenge and harvest while keeping an eye out for something to shoot.

All of the permaculture principles were there waiting to be respected. I learnt so much from my parents and their attitudes. They were my first teachers in pioneering a small hands-on isolated farm. But I also learnt a lot more from the raw primal landscape of Australia, its seasons and cycles and later in life from its indigenous peoples.

Another very fortunate experience was turning up in London in the early 1960s. Psychedelics completely shattered my reductionist world view. A whole new world

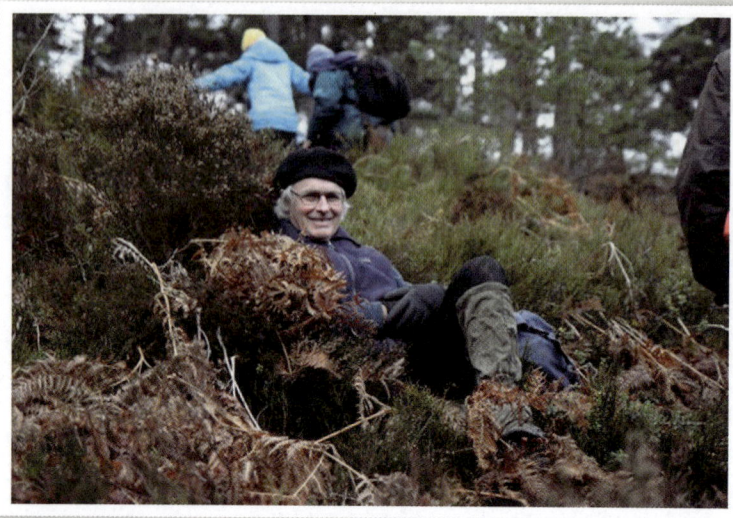

Craig Gibsone

of creativity and collaboration opened up. So intense was the experience that I went and spent three years in a Tibetan meditation centre, my first real connection with an indigenous culture and their world view.

Buddhism brought new insights along with the Way of the Tao. It was there that I had my first taste of living in community and met two of the founders of Findhorn, a Western Mystery School, who spoke of a new age of secular enlightenment where spirituality was integrated into daily life and co-creation with nature was imperative.

Going to visit this community was a big surprise. The founders had all done their inner work and used their intuitive abilities to guide them. It was a bunch of old caravans surrounded by windswept sand dunes, situated on a disused World War Two military base. Concrete parking bays for aircraft and dilapidated war time temporary buildings were the main features.

They had built a simple wooden shed used solely for meditation and in that simple wooden shed I felt my heart opening to the soul of humanity and Gaia. Thus began a journey of spiritual and appreciative inquiry into the mystery of being a human, at this time in our evolutionary journey, with a dedicated group of people. Findhorn became vortices of energy absorbing the best of human practices while growing and building community.

For the last 47 years I have been involved in implementing this vision. The founders were good teachers, as they said follow your heart, listen to that intuitive voice and practice daily. Spend time listening to nature, observing, sensing, listening, together in small groups, listening to the pulse of life in the community around you, listening to the beat of our social interactions as a species, and listen to this Earth. She has drawn us forth and will guide us into the indefinite future if we listen and observe our interactions with life.

Half way through this journey I found myself building and living in a small whiskey barrel house surrounded by an experimental wild garden. It was when I was asked if it could be used for a practical work session on Permaculture that my eyes opened. It was then that many threads came together, and Permaculture became a language to complement all the spiritual lessons I had learned in monasteries, ashrams, communities, indigenous peoples and from being born in the bush.

As we have written earlier, a key practice of Permaculture is Observation – observing your life style and how it is affecting the state of the planet – and then there is sitting still and observing how your feelings, your emotions, your state of mind and your spiritual well-being are also affecting everything.

These two major themes in my life come together into a seamless holistic relationship. They enhance one another, problems become solutions and everything gardens. There is an unlimited yield as one works with nature and the nature of one's self, minimizing your efforts while maximizing the effect. You will be guided to make the connections and to enhance the co-creation potential.

PART ONE

Earthcare

*Look at the abundance of nature, of the beauty all around you,
and recognize Me in everything. How many times during the
day as you walk to and fro do you look at the wonders all around
you and give thanks for everything?*
— EILEEN CADDY

Earthcare is one of the ethical principles in the Permaculture philosophy. There is no definite order in the three ethics. It would be more helpful to regard them as three legs on a stool. Each is vital for the stool to function, but no one ethic is more important than any other.

Permaculture as a design system is based on natural systems. It is about working with nature, not against it – not using natural resources unnecessarily or at a rate at which they cannot be replaced. Permaculture also means using outputs from one system as inputs for another (vegetable peelings as compost, for example), and so minimizing wastage. Sometimes we define Permaculture as a "Dialogue with Nature" meaning that we work together, making small changes and observing their effects, using the feedback we get to adjust further small changes.

In this section we shall look at soil, plants, farming, building and technology. In all these areas our actions, in supplying our needs, meet the planet in a myriad of ways. This is the "edge" between humans and the environment, and in fact this is where we experience ourselves as part of nature, part of the natural cycles that wheel all around us, day in and day out.

In many of these meeting places, our relationship with nature has become totally dysfunctional, leading to pollution, soil degradation, ruined landscapes and uninhabitable regions. Places where our actions lead to sickness, disease and death, for people, for other animals and birds, and plant and insect life. Sometimes we need extreme conditions to tell us that we need to change. Sometimes we need reminding of our dependence upon nature.

Global awareness is reaching new levels and Permaculture is one response to this crisis, a response that gives us hope for the future, based on creating positive change for the better.

One very positive aspect that is currently sweeping through the Permaculture world is sometimes referred to as "Earth Jurisprudence". Human beings have defined legal rights, and even though many countries don't respect them as well as they should, these rights have been legally enshrined by most countries, and can be enforced through international courts.

The Universal Declaration of the Rights of Mother Earth gives our natural ecosystems legal rights and definitions. Lawyers may represent Mother Earth in international courts, and groups of people who infringe these rights may be brought to trial and convicted. This is ground-breaking work, being followed up right now by a small network of dedicated individuals. As these changes are brought into use, we may well see big changes in the way we farm our soils, build our houses and in the kinds of technology we may employ.

This section of our book explores some of the implications and looks at some of the possibilities that this kind of thinking will generate.

CHAPTER TWO

Soil and Plants

I see the mycelium as the Earth's natural Internet,
a consciousness with which we might be able to communicate.
Through cross-species interfacing, we may one day exchange
information with these sentient cellular networks.

— *PAUL STAMETS*

Eileen and Peter Caddy and Dorothy Maclean all followed a disciplined spiritual practice for many years before they came to live at Findhorn, and they continued their regular meditation times when they came to live at the caravan park.

In May 1963 Dorothy Maclean received an insight from within as she meditated:

"The forces of nature are something to be felt into, to be reached out to. One of the jobs for you as my free child is to sense the Nature forces such as the wind, to perceive its essence and purpose for me, and to be positive and harmonize with that essence."

When Dorothy shared this insight with Peter, his idea was to apply to their fledgling garden what Dorothy learned from the forces of nature. Dorothy then received this insight:

"Yes, you can cooperate in the garden. Begin by thinking about the nature spirits, the higher overlighting nature spirits, and tune into them. That will be so unusual as to draw their interest here. They will be overjoyed to find some members of the human race eager for their help."

Angels, Devas and Elemental Beings

Dorothy first attuned to the garden pea. As her communication with the forces of nature developed, Dorothy realized that she was in contact not with the spirit of an individual plant, but with the "overlighting" being of the species, which was the consciousness holding the archetypal design of the species and the blueprint for its highest potential. She was experiencing a formless energy field for which there is no word.

The closest word to convey the joy and purity that these beings emanated was the inaccurate word 'angel' (which in the West is full of form), and her first thought was to call them that. However, the Sanskrit term "deva", meaning "shining one" seemed more accurate and freer of cultural associations.

In practice, she uses both words, although neither word is adequate. Peter and Dorothy applied the insights of the meditations to their work in the garden, and through this the Findhorn garden flourished. These were the first steps in the Findhorn Community's co-creation with nature.

In 1966 Peter Caddy met Robert Ogilvie Crombie, or Roc, as he is often called. Roc's ability to communicate with elemental beings is a well-documented part of the community's history, and he was an important influence on the development of the community as a place where the role of nature in ordinary life was brought to the forefront of consciousness.

This special relationship with the beings of nature continues to be practised by some of the people working in the community's gardens today, but not by everyone. Before most activities such as cooking, painting, healing, or starting work in a department for the day, there is usually an attunement invoking active cooperation with an overlighting consciousness. This helps to align our actions and unfold the highest potential available in that particular task.

Awareness and cooperation with the forces of nature at this level are an important support and balance for the more exoteric, rational and scientific ecological approach of our ecovillage development and education. It is important to recognize and emphasize the intrinsic value of nature to truly form a cooperative partnership.

It is the combination of these approaches that allows the Findhorn Foundation community to give its unique gift towards the sustainability of humanity and all of life.

> *The devas, who at first seemed to be far-off beings, through a joyous communion grew into close companions until eventually they made me realize that they, like the kingdom of heaven, are within.*
>
> — *DOROTHY MACLEAN*

The Inner Life of Plants

It's hard to shift our thinking over to accepting that plants have a rich inner life. That they feel, experience and communicate with each other and with us. With our materialist upbringing we react negatively, we dismiss it. But as good Permaculturalists we might spend some time observing nature and asking some questions.

Some plants lack a support system, choosing (do they have a choice?) to use other plants such as trees, or combinations of sticks that we build for them, to climb upon. If we move these sticks, the vine will change its course, looking for alternatives. How does it decide to do that? It has no eyes that we can see, how does it "sense" the support that was there and now is no longer there but moved somewhere else?

Vines of all sorts will seek out support systems, growing through or around obstructions to get there. Clearly they don't have our senses, our eyes, our touch or sense of smell or hearing. Or do they? Do they possess other senses that we can only dream about? Do they possess senses that we don't even know exist?

The behaviour of plants is only beginning to be discovered and researched upon. After filling their book *The Secret Life of Plants* with such stories, and raising countless questions, Peter Tompkins and Christopher Bird concluded:

"Plants are capable of intent: they can stretch towards, or seek out, what they want in ways as mysterious as the most fantastic creations of romance."

Giving plants their own space.

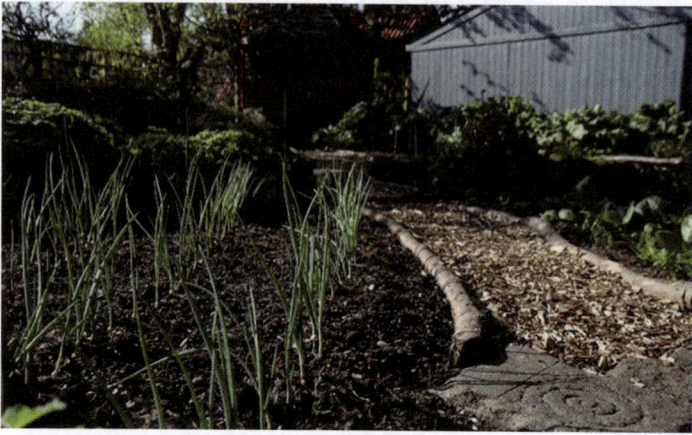

Springtime in the Original Garden of the Findhorn Foundation.

Plants possess attributes that we know nothing about. They communicate with their environment, they respond to their surroundings, they find moisture and nutrients, and have means of recording and transmitting information. Some of this we have learnt to read, so we can count the age of a tree by its rings, or the passage of day and night by the opening and closing of flowers.

But we have only touched the tip of the iceberg, and there remains a vast and unexplored territory awaiting those who want to delve deeper.

There are many other influences that interact with plants than just the passing of the years or the rhythms of day and night. The moon cycle with its waxing and waning is reflected in the growth of plants, something that many gardeners will confirm. Biodynamic gardeners will check out the positions of the stars and the zodiac, and they plant, cultivate and harvest accordingly.

These observations are there to be seen, but they are subtle, and they require deep observation, detailed recording and documentation, and the backup of other observers with whom to compare and contrast findings.

In our transition from the old mechanistic paradigm to the holistic one, we find that there is much more to plants than we had thought. It fits in with the cutting edge discoveries of quantum physics that human beings and plants have a two-way communication when observing each other, and that plants have communication systems that interact with a vast constellation of other species and varieties.

Tompkins and Bird conclude their book by writing:

"... plants are living, breathing, communicating creatures, endowed with personality, and the attributes of soul."

In his book on trees, Fred Hageneder writes about Lawrence Edwards, who did extensive research on the subtle pulsating movements of leaf buds on deciduous trees. What he found was that there was a striking correlation between the pulse of the buds and the alignments of the Earth, the Moon and other planets. Not only that, but different species pulsed together with different planets. The oak corresponded with Mars, beech with Saturn and birch with Venus.

Lawrence published his meticulous research in 1993 in the book *The Vortex of Life*. These discoveries may not in themselves prove or disprove anything, but they do open up a number of questions which in the spirit of Permaculture may lead us to a deeper understanding of the patterns in nature. As we have noted before, Permaculture is about asking questions much more than giving precise answers.

Questions open up our minds, allowing for surprising new solutions to emerge.

- How can I find out more about how plants perceive and behave?
- Can I find patterns in plant behaviour that might lead me to be able to predict certain growth cycles?
- How can I work together with these patterns to design more stable, abundant and sustainable ecologies?

Soil Mycelium Networks

In a sense, plants can be seen as an extrusion of the soil, a manifestation of the hidden life under the turf. This matrix from which the plants emerge we call soil, and this soil contains unexplored territory that we are only just beginning to discern.

There are so many millions of living entities in just a teaspoon of this soil that we don't know half of their names yet. But what we do know is that they are living together and producing an abundance for us that we are totally dependent upon. It seems that some of the organisms that keeps this soil living are the mycelia, the fungi, that break down complex organic molecules into simpler ones that then become available for plants to absorb as nutrients.

Research shows that these fungi are able to sense what is going on in the environment. They feel a branch falling to the ground in the forest, and the footsteps of an animal on the prairie. Information is passed rapidly throughout vast underground networks, occasionally covering many square miles of forest or savannah.

A predatory intruder, for instance a disease in a forest, will attack one or two trees, and very quickly, all the trees of that species will respond with defensive strategies. We humans can only build similar systems with highly advanced, expensive and complex technologies. The mycelia do this silently and seemingly without using any energy. We have a lot to learn!

We need to tap into that ancient knowledge. We need to be able to listen and to learn how this is done. By working with nature, by learning from nature's patterns, we can switch from being an element that destroys and pollutes, to being an element that enhances and develops our environment, creating more abundance than we will ever know what to do with.

In fact, research is showing us that we can use many of the qualities and attributes of different mycelia to break down some of the toxins and pollutants that we are currently throwing out into nature. By studying the smallest details of soil, mycelia and other organisms, we may be able to learn how to deal with the wholeness of life on this planet.

Indeed it would be wise of us to check how our activities are impacting upon the carrying capacity of our planet. One of the patterns that we can observe in nature is that when an organism exceeds the carrying capacity of its environment, its support systems will inevitably fail, leading to collapse.

Perelandra

Perelandra celebrates the power of the individual and is geared to the individual and his or her quest to live in environmentally friendly ways by including nature's intelligence. Our current crisis was created by each of us acting independently and establishing a personal and professional lifestyle that was environmentally deaf, dumb and blind.

The needed coordination between governments and industry to turn this crisis around will never succeed if we as individuals don't join in the efforts. If the same number of individuals who created the problem focused on what they need to do on the personal level to live an environmentally conscious life, we could turn the global problems around in an amazingly short time.

Machaelle Wright, who founded Perelandra at Findhorn and subsequently took it to the USA, believes in the power of the individual and in the importance of our acting responsibly as individuals without waiting for the right leader or group. It's the power of the individual that leads the way.

Now imagine what we individuals could accomplish if we teamed up with the greatest authority in the field of balance — nature — to help us personally to make the best decisions for improving our lives and our planet.

Perelandra is all about giving individuals the information and tools for creating just such a partnership for addressing every aspect of our life and work. (See Web References, page 171, for further reading.)

Plant and Human Symbiosis

We breathe in oxygen that combines with the carbon in our bodies, and we exhale carbon dioxide. If we carried on doing this the atmosphere of our planet would gradually change. The composition of this atmosphere is balanced by plants that inhale carbon dioxide and exhale oxygen, so plants are not just food for us, they are also partners with us in maintaining our environment.

In us, the oxygen we take in is absorbed by our blood, which in turn releases carbon dioxide to be exhaled. In the plant, the sap takes up carbon dioxide and releases oxygen. Blood and sap are two liquids that complement each other. If we are looking for patterns here, as we should be when we are using Permaculture thinking, we might perceive a certain symmetry between the blood in our veins and the sap in plants.

We are complex organisms, composed of elements, some of which are animal-like, others plant-like and yet others are minerals. Teeth and bones are obvious examples of minerals in our body. The digestive and breathing systems are very plant-like, they seem to have their own slow metabolism, over which we have only limited control. Obviously we are animals, the human animal, and much of our behaviour is controlled by our instincts rather than our rationality, though there do seem to be times when we can exercise our free will. We have a sense of relationship to the wider cosmos and a connection to the sacred.

When we were young we used to play a guessing game called, "Animal, vegetable or mineral?" We may want to bring this back into our Permaculture Design Courses. Categorizing the contents of our world in this way helps us to understand our world. In this progression from mineral, through plants to animals we also perceive a process of evolution as has happened on Earth.

Our world began as a lump of matter (matter – mater – mother) spinning in space. Gradually conditions conspired to create life, and from the algae or whatever exhibited the very first stirrings of something living, came plant-like phenomena. Only much later did some kind of animals emerge, completely changing the face of the Earth.

We human beings clearly ascribe our origins to a long succession of animal forms, but we are a pretty recent phenomenon, a million years at the very most. On the geological scale, we were born yesterday.

If we observe minerals, plants, animals and humans, most of us would agree that there are a number of characteristics that give us a clear division into different categories. Minerals appear lifeless. Their ability to move of their own accord is severely limited. Changes occurring in minerals take extremely long times.

Plants, on the other hand, show signs of life, even though they don't move very much. They have life cycles, they respond to external stimuli. They repair themselves when damaged, sometimes. They can be extremely complex. Moving up the succession to animals, we find here creatures that can move, are even more complex than plants, but share with the plant world the ability to repair themselves, and exhibit lifecycles.

It may seem that they show signs of free will, but in most cases this is still pretty limited, and instincts play a larger part than rational decisions based on thought processes.

◈

This last feature can be found in humans. Some of us, some of the time, seem to exercise rational thought, and our actions are occasionally based upon this. Most people would agree that we have a certain degree of free will, even if we don't use it all the time. We certainly have an awareness of ourselves that we seldom recognize in animals, though neither of us have swum with dolphins or had any interaction with the great apes. It seems that many of those who do, discover a deeper connection with these creatures.

If one of the aspects of evolution is to produce ever more complex forms of life, a pattern that most of us would clearly perceive in nature, then the addition of consciousness would correspond to yet another step up the evolutionary ladder.

However we might generally describe ourselves, intelligent or stupid, there can be no doubt that some of us, some of the time, exercise our consciousness in truly miraculous ways. The history of all culture is the story of great achievements in art, in music and in thought.

More recently, with the spread of reading and writing, literature has become something that exercises millions of people. The rise of digital media and the internet has produced for the first time ever, the beginnings of a truly global culture.

It would seem sensible to design a global culture that solves our problems rather than creating them. That's what Permaculture is all about.

PERSONAL STORY · GILAD MARGALIT

The Joy Of Composting

I VIVIDLY REMEMBER the first feeling of realizing that every choice I make in my life has infinite ripples and consequences in the world. I realized I have an ecological and social footprint that has a negative affect on people and ecosystems. Although this feeling gradually took shape and form over the years, the basic realization felt like falling into an endless void of responsibility, a paralysis by analysis of the consciousness…

In my early activist years, this feeling made me very dramatic about every choice: how to travel, where to live, what to buy, how to brush my teeth, and even from what materials to build a natural building… I got ideologically religious about it!

But over time, the sheer mass of information collapsed onto itself in order to create a deeper void: a spiritual one. A void in my consciousness that was gravitating deeper answers for doing permaculture in my life. A void in my heart and soul was revealed, reflecting to me that no matter how much I tried to minimize my ecological footprint, it had nothing to do with real happiness.

It was like a strange kind of materialism that never really made me happy and satisfied.

Through a long process of self-inquiry and learning from people like Joanna Macy and Bill Plotkin my perception shifted from chronic panic and rightfulness to a deeper understanding of interconnectedness. Instead of seeing actions from the narrow prism of judgment and blame I began appreciating my choices from a more mindful perspective: gratitude for the beauty and complexity of life, and finding joy and peace in doing the most positive action I can in every choice I make.

"When I am connected to this infinite root in my soul, I practice spiritual permaculture."

The first time I had a successful compost pile was a transformative and powerful experience! I lived on a farm in southern Oregon that had a commercial kitchen. The leftovers were thrown away to a fenced pile, just to rot away in the cold and rainy winter. When I arrived to the site the scene was awful: grey, slimy organic matter stinking and fermenting. As a young Permaculture enthusiast, just graduated from my first PDC (Permaculture Design Course), I decided that this was a task for me!

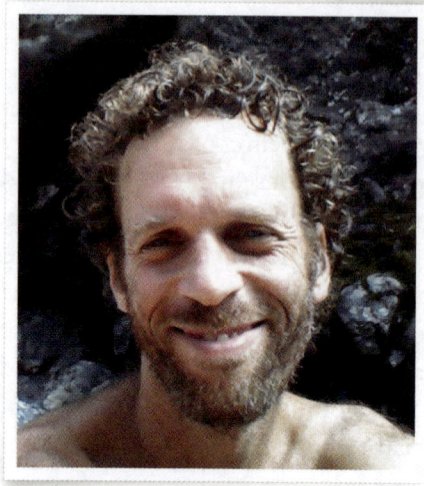

Gilad Margalit

I spent the next few weeks reading and learning about composting and implementing the theory into practice: taking every bit of dry and dark pile of leaves, straw and shredded wood and mixing it in, mainly by foot (with rain-boots on.) and or with a fork.

I inserted perforated tubes into the pile and sheltered it from the rain. And then the magic happened. I remember coming back to check on the pile a few days later and smelled the warm and healthy air of a well cooking pile! The temperature meter and my bare hands concluded my observations: Success!

Thirteen years later, I am still excited about composting. I experimented and learned many techniques and now enjoy lush winter greens that are growing on a composted mix of humanure, worm castings, and goat manure.

However, the greatest thing I learned from composting is not the technique. It is the essence of energetic transformation and systems' interrelationships.

These universal and eternal principles, that I have also learned from many other disciplines and philosophies like Taoism, Aikido, Buddhism, Yoga, Co-counselling and Spiral Dynamics, are a mega-pattern in all realms of life.

If we say that compost is an essential element in the growth of every healthy permaculture garden then I may add that the ability to transform and "compost" inner and inter-human dynamics is the foundation for the growth of every healthy person, family and community – that are the second foundation for a permanent culture.

Over those years I've built many gardens and nowadays I realize that these gardens will flourish or decay depending on the level of "spiritual composting" I am practicing in my inner landscapes and human ecological systems, a far greater challenge then just maintaining the compost pile in my back yard…

Happy composting!

NOTE: *Gilad Margalit teaches Permaculture in Israel, is an active member of the Israeli Permaculture Association, and has mentored several diploma candidates over the last few years. He lives at Kadita Ecovillage and is working on getting Ecovillages to become a recognized part of rural Israel.*

CHAPTER THREE

Gardening and Farming

The ultimate goal of farming is not the growing of crops,
but the cultivation and perfection of human beings.
— MASANOBU FUKUOKA: *The One Straw Revolution.*

At first glance it might seem that farming and gardening were pretty physical tasks, bound up with tools, with iron and steel, and the expenditure of hard work. Permaculture tries to do away with some of the hard work, by working together with nature, letting nature do as much of the work as possible.

So we let the earthworms and other soil organisms dig our soil instead of breaking our own backs using shovels, and we try to design water systems that use gravity flow rather than pumps and muscle power to move the water around.

Edward Hyams in his book *Soil and Civilization* defines two sets of tools employed in farming. One set is what we just described, the physical tools of steel and wood. The other is a set of psychological tools that are the methods, traditions and techniques that we have worked out over time, using our thinking combined with experience.

This set of tools he again divides into two, the intellectual and the spiritual. The former is pretty obvious; we act, we observe, we think rationally and we modify our

A network of interconnectedness.

actions. This is classic Permaculture practice, the use of observation, the dialogue with nature; "observe and interact".

The spiritual aspect is interesting to us as a departure into new ways of thinking, to embed Permaculture firmly into the new paradigm. Spiritual aspects of farming involve following traditions of thinking, in the old days of considering the needs and ways of the spirits working in the land; today being aware of the interconnectedness of all things.

Biodynamics

Biodynamic gardening and farming has been doing just this for nearly a century, since Rudolf Steiner gave his first series of lectures on the subject at Koberwitz in Silesia, now Poland, in 1924. There are several main themes in Biodynamic agriculture:

- Communicating with the elemental beings of the plants and the soil.
- Cultivating the soil and the plants together with the cosmic rhythms.
- Regarding the farm or the garden as a whole organism.
- Self development of the gardener or farmer through working with soil and plants.
- Producing nutritious food that nourishes both body and soul.

In addition, there is an understanding that soil has its own life, its own vitality, and that it behaves as an organism. It lives off nutrients that either are delivered to it or that it finds; it has a metabolism that digests and produces, and it gives forth an abundance of captured energy, in a multitude of forms, including foodstuffs for other plants, for insects, animals and humans. Biodynamics raises a series of questions regarding the soil and our relationship to it:

- Does the soil itself have a memory?
- Is it a living organism revealing a life of the spirit as well as the physical life of digestion and excretion?
- How can we connect to the consciousness of the micro soil community and use this connection to design more productive, happier and fulfilling gardens and farms?

The usual round of physical factors such as soil, minerals, water and climate are clearly important. In addition, Biodynamics also considers forces acting upon the Earth from outside. The sun is obvious, we can all observe the opening and closing of flowers from day to night. The moon is less obvious, but most experienced gardeners notice subtle differences in growth rates between the waxing and the waning of the moon.

Other factors are more subtle, but careful and mindful use of the Biodynamic calendars such as Maria Thun's, will usually lead to better quality produce in larger quantities, free from pests and diseases. This will come as no surprise to anyone familiar with the latest findings in physics that show that all matter is interrelated and displays a constant and instantaneous flow of information.

Similarly, being aware of the energy in all things, including stone and plant, is not a big step away from regarding this energy as a form of spirit. As we saw earlier, this can often be a semantic difference. Combining the energy that is in all things with the previous idea of all matter (energy) being interrelated and inter-aware, we are very close to working together with the elemental beings of the plants, gardening with the devas.

This is not an extraordinary statement, but just another way of acknowledging that some people have "green thumbs", something that many people are aware of, and many of us have experienced in neighbours, friends or family members. Or in ourselves.

Self-development of the Farmer

Take a simple farmer… who meditates on all sorts of things during the winter nights. And indeed he arrives at a way of acquiring spiritual knowledge, though he may not be able to express it… As he is walking through the fields it is suddenly there. He knows what to do, and he tries it out. I lived among farmers when I was young, and I saw this happen again and again. It really does happen.

— *RUDOLF STEINER, from a lecture at Koberwits in June 1924.*
Translated in Spiritual Ecology. Ed Matthew Barton. Rudolf Steiner Press, 2008.

Biodynamic gardeners and farmers form associations in many countries of the world. When they get together, part of their time is taken up by the usual things that a specific interest would lead them to do; sharing experiences, knowledge and know- how. In addition, they spend time working on self-development, studying texts, discussing their meanings, and some groups meditate or think together, sometimes with words, sometimes using silence.

Both instincts and intuition are regarded as important qualities that could be further developed. So Biodynamics is not just a better way of growing carrots, it's also a way of growing better people; more fulfilled, more aware.

We would like to make a distinction between instinct and intuition, as they play a part in the dialogue between spirituality and Permaculture. Instinct is best seen in those with a green thumb, it is a natural ability to grow things, a gift, while intuition is more reflective, observing, sensing, being still and waiting for solutions to arise. Both are important and lead to a healthier interaction with the ecosystem.

In our endeavour to design a better world, and looking for solutions to the challenges that face us, finding partners is a valuable exercise. Combining Permaculture and Biodynamics is a win–win situation, utilizing the wisdom that has been built up from nearly a century of Biodynamic experience with the smart solutions that Permaculture has developed over the last generation.

One Indian farmer summed it up elegantly:

"With Permaculture we build soil, and with Biodynamics we grow plants. Both are necessary."

The Findhorn Foundation gardens today integrate Biodynamics, Permaculture and sound organic gardening techniques and are most of all a great place to grow people.

Returning the Social to Agriculture

For many thousands of years, we lived in farming villages, worked the land, and celebrated the round of the seasons as part of our religious, spiritual and cultural life. Jan lived for many years on a kibbutz in the centre of Israel, and on the ancient city mound, only a half hour walk away, was found one of the very first pieces of written Hebrew, dating back about 3,000 years.

This was called the Gezer Calendar, and can be seen in the Archaeological Museum in Istanbul. It is indeed an agricultural calendar, marking the passing of the seasons, something that was familiar to the members of the kibbutz so many millennia later.

Today, with just over half the people on this planet living in cities, many of us have lost this connection to the rhythms of the year and the seasons. And the loss has not been so positive. In doing so, we are cut off from nature, it's become harder for us to appreciate what an abundance she gives us, and we have the archetypal situation where children think that milk comes from boxes in the supermarket rather than from cows being milked.

One strategy that is developing a new relationship between the grower and the consumer is the Community Supported Agriculture (CSA) movement, which is experiencing large growth rates in the western world. A variety of forms have been

The Cullerne Gardens in Findhorn - part of one of the first CSA schemes in the UK.

developed, ranging from the more casual Farmer's Markets, to groups of people in the city buying a farm and hiring a farmer to grow food for them.

Most CSAs consist of a membership group who commit to buying a box of kitchen-ready seasonal vegetables that they receive each week or month.

One of the interesting side effects of CSAs is the social effect. Many CSA farms have open days when members are encouraged to gather together with their children, and celebrate some aspect of the year. Harvest festivals are a big hit here. Children see farms at work, discover how crops and animals are tended, and get to taste safe, chemical free food straight off the land.

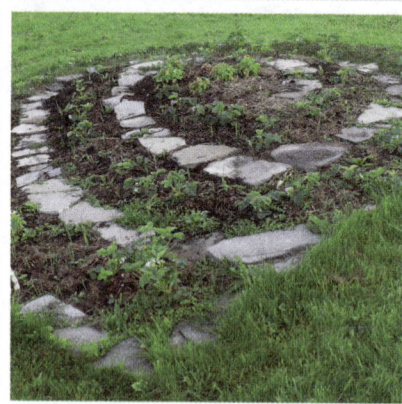

Flat spiral vegetable garden in the Arctic, from a PDC in Norway, 2012.

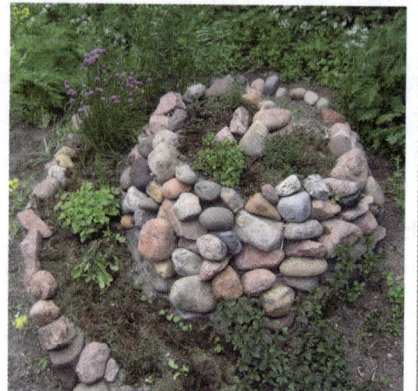

Herb spiral from a Norwegian Steiner School, 2004.

This celebration of the seasons and of nature's abundance is not necessarily a spiritual exercise in itself, but is part of the hidden side of Permaculture design. Not only do we get good nutritious food, but in addition we find ways of getting together socially that do not cost a lot of money, and are not subject to exploitation. Bringing the social back into agriculture is in itself a way of creating a more aware and contented community.

Devas, Nature Spirits and Good Compost

Working with the land in a conscious way has been a key element in the evolution of the Findhorn Foundation community since the earliest days. Indeed it was probably the aspect of the community that attracted more interest than any other. The three founders received spiritual guidance that they should start a garden on the sand dune where their caravan was located (as it still is), in spite of the lack of soil.

There began a synthesis of approaches, which is still significant today. They brought together a spiritual source of information through Dorothy Maclean's communication with spiritual beings she called the devas of each particular plant species. They also absorbed the latest ideas in organic farming as researched by Peter Caddy as well as information from experienced local gardeners.

The result was superb vegetables coming out of this inhospitable sand dune and people coming from all over the world to see them. Today the Findhorn gardeners mostly do not claim such direct communication as Dorothy received, but are all committed to developing the intuitive side of their relationship to plants.

Dorothy, still, constantly, confirms the importance of everyone developing their own understanding and intuition in ways that are natural to them.

Sustainable Yogic Agriculture

In January 2015 Jan visited the Rajasthan College of Agriculture, a department of the Maharana Pratap University of Agriculture and Technology in Udaipur. Dr. Anila Doshi, researcher in mushrooms, and Dr. Amit Trivedi, Associate Professor in organic farming, told him how the traditional Ayurvedic medicine requires extracts from organically grown plants.

They estimated that Indian agriculture is about 30 to 40% organic, and within tribal areas almost totally. 15 to 20% of their students are committed to organic growing, and at the university they are using Biodynamic methods. They talked a great deal about Sustainable Yogic Agriculture, which is based on traditional, or-

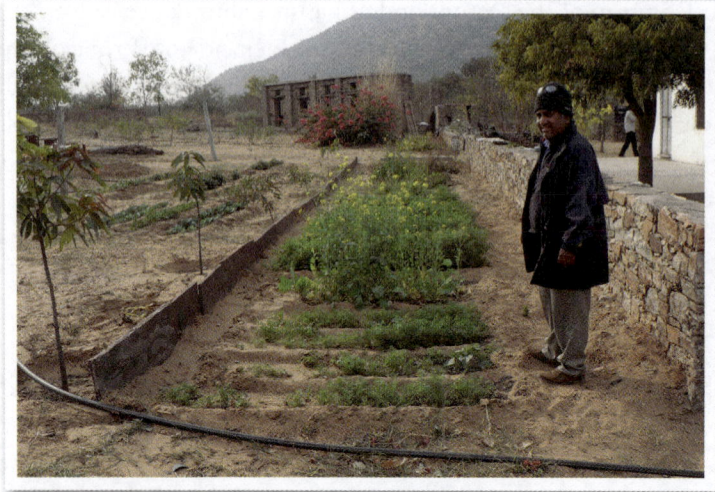

Apal Agrawal applying Permaculture techniques to Neem Tree Farm
in Rajasthan, India.

ganic, yogic farming. There are spiritual inputs, mantra chants for seeds to maintain energy and meditation for the farmers. It struck us that in India there is a much more open and accepting attitude to the spiritual side of existence, and that western agricultural researchers might gain a great deal from collaborating with their Indian colleagues. (See Web References, page 171, for further reading.)

The Findhorn Garden

In the early 1970s Peter Caddy observed that we had stopped growing vegetables and started growing people. The Gardens of Findhorn gave birth to the group processes of People Care and we began to harvest from the rich and diverse fields of human interaction by blending spiritual beliefs and practices with those of psychology.

Psyche and soul became partners in creating tools for the transformation of consciousness, where we compost our pain, fear and anxieties, opening up to the vast fields of awareness, sensing ourselves as one being, one heart, one mind.

The garden became a jungle, the jungle a garden, Permaculture blooms upon the compost heap of impermanence.

The story of the Findhorn garden with its 40-lb. cabbages and other marvels, might have seemed whimsical fantasy were there not growing testimony that something truly extraordinary was happening here. Professor R. Lindsay Robb of the Soil Association was one of a number of authorities impressed by the vitality and vibrancy of the Findhorn garden. He wrote in his evaluation:

Abundance in Findhorn's Original Garden.

"The vigour, health and bloom of the plants in this garden at mid-winter on land which is almost barren, powdery sand cannot be explained by the moderate dressings of compost, nor indeed by the application of any known cultural methods of organic husbandry. There are other factors and they are vital ones."

— *Faces of Findhorn. Findhorn Publications, 1980.*

Are Landscapes Alive?

Landscapes in their wholeness, including all the elements; geology, plants, animals and human-made features, can be considered as whole living organisms. Andreas Suchantke in his book *Eco-Geography* comments that it is only a short step from looking at the landscape as an "ecosystem" to looking at it as an "organism".

By doing so, we gain a new and much more dynamic appreciation of the processes at work. He defines a number of characteristics of a living organism, such as respiration, thermal regulation and nutrition, and looks for them in the landscape. Respiration he finds in the continuing gas exchange between oxygen and carbon dioxide, between plants and animals.

Thermal regulation consists of the solar gain during the day being ameliorated by the water in the landscape, both in the form of standing or running water, and in the water-carrying capacities of plants, especially trees, and of course the soil itself.

Nutrition happens continuously, as various substances are endlessly recycled by

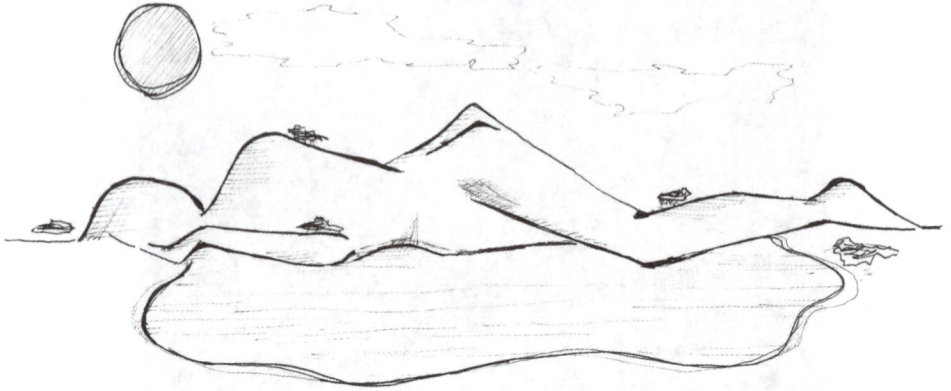

Are landscapes alive?

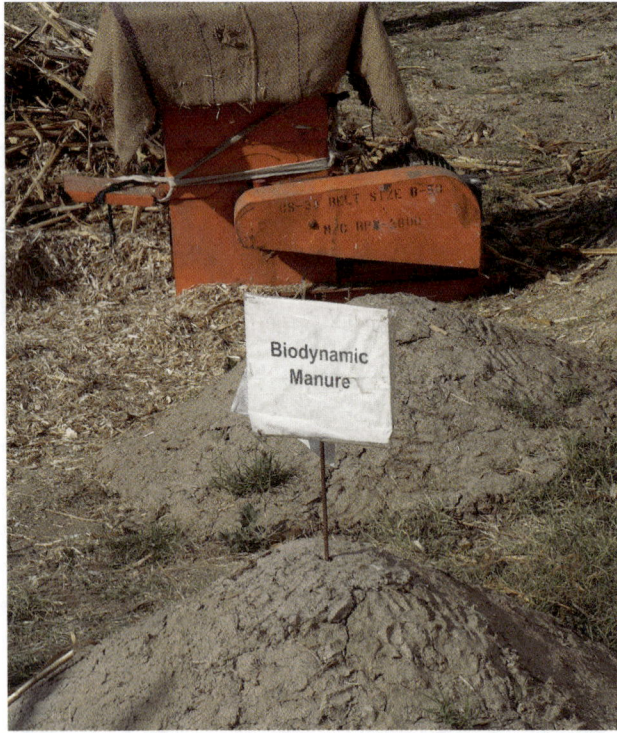

Biodynamic manure at Maharana Pratap University of Agriculture and Technology, Udaipur, Rajasthan, India.

the process of plant and animal growth, and the breakdown of organic matter. In addition to balancing the temperature, water serves as a circulation system, bringing nutrients and information to every part of the organism.

Suchantke compares the birds to the sensory aspects of a living being, the herds of herbivores to the metabolic system, and the predators to the balancing rhythmic system of the lungs and heart. In this sense landscapes may be called synergetic communities, and compared to living creatures such as ourselves.

This view of landscapes as living beings is not necessarily a "truth", but gives us a picture, an image, which may help us to see the landscape in a different light, and to design changes that we want to implement. In this way it is a tool, a thinking device, which if it helps, is by definition helpful, and if not, can be laid aside for future use.

Ecological Restoration

Not only must the concept of wilderness, and human attitude to it, radically shift; our generation should make major efforts to reverse the damage to the environment that has already taken place. Nature is always in dynamic equilibrium, in a multitude of constant cycles of birth, death and rebirth.

However, this natural process is being prevented in most situations throughout the world by the scale and intensity of human activities. In many cases we need to help restoration take place.

Compost helps to bring life back to the soil and the landscape.

In Glen Affric, Scotland.

If the human race is to continue to exist on planet Earth we need to seek not only to conserve and protect it but also to take into account the interconnectedness of all things; to seek to understand its complexity and above all relearn to honour and love all parts of planet Earth.

Making A Difference

MY OWN EXPERIENCE of working practically with the restoration of the Caledonian Forest for over ten years has shown me that ecological restoration is not just about helping to reconnect the strands in the web of life. It also helps to reconnect the people carrying out restoration work with some of the most important things in our lives.

It helps to reconnect us with our power as individuals to make a difference in the world and to reconnect us with hope for the future. I believe that together we can all change the suicidal course of our present culture, and create a future in which humanity once again lives in harmony with the rest of Nature on a healthy planet with restored ecosystems. However, it's up to all of us to make it happen and we have to start now.

There is one further factor that gives me hope for the future – the irrepressible life force of Nature. I've experienced it directly in Scotland, when I've found naturally regenerating Scots pine seedlings, kilometres from any possible seed source, in areas where we are seeking to restore the Caledonian forest.

The forests will come back, as soon as circumstances (and people) allow a few seedlings to gain a root-hold. The wounds on the Earth will heal, and if we actively assist in this, we can accelerate the restoration process.

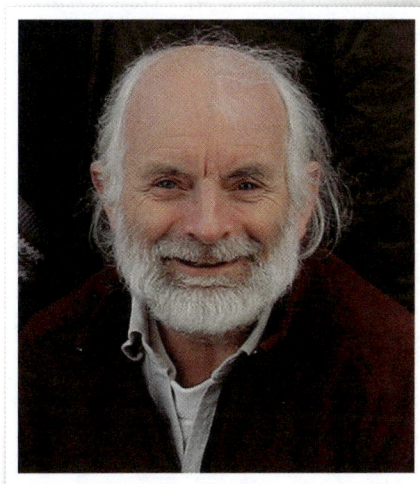

Alan Watson Featherstone

NOTE: *Alan Watson Featherstone, the founding director and inspiration behind Trees for Life, has been a member of the Findhorn Foundation Community since 1978. He was the main organiser of a conference called One Earth: A Call to Action in 1986 which led to his founding of the Trees for Life Programme.*

Trees for Life is an independent registered Scottish Charity associated with the Findhorn Foundation, and as such is very much a part of the vision of the Findhorn Community as an Ecovillage.

Trees for Life holds the awareness of and involvement with "connection to nature through the wilderness" for the Findhorn Community, with the main long-term aim to return an area over 2,500 square kilometres to a condition of wild natural forest. With Scotland's native forest cover being only 1% of its former size this work is essential.

Trees for Life acts locally but holds a global awareness for the diminishing natural environment. Trees for Life owns the 10,000 acre (4,000 hectare) Dundreggan Estate in Glen Moriston, Scotland, and also works in partnership with government agencies, private landowners and other conservation groups, to restore and regenerate the Caledonian Forest.

The target area surrounds and includes Glen Affric, one of the best remnants of the old forest in Scotland. This area in the north-central Highlands is largely roadless and almost completely uninhabited, and is therefore one of the very few large tracts of land in Scotland which have the potential to be restored to a wilderness state.

Containing mountains and lochs as well as formerly forested land, it includes all the necessary habitats to support the species of wildlife that we aim to reintroduce in due course.

(See Web References, page 171, for further reading.)

CHAPTER FOUR

Water

*When the doors of your heart are closed and the flow of love
and light ceases, your whole life becomes stagnant,
and nothing lives in a stagnant pool. That is why you have consciously to keep those doors wide open and draw from Me,
the source of all life, all the time, so that your heart never
at any time becomes dried up and stagnant. A stream that ceases
to draw its supply from its source dries up.*
— *EILEEN CADDY*

*"Human beings gradually lost the knowledge and experience
of the spiritual nature of water, until at last they came to treat
it merely as a substance and a means of transmitting energy."*
— *THEODOR SCHWENK: Sensitive Chaos.*

Water is the womb of life. We spent the first nine months of our lives in a wa-
tery world and our bodies are over 60% water. The planet's surface is largely
water. It affects everything we do from growing food to washing our bodies, and was
one of our first Holy Sacraments.

It carries our emotions and expresses our feelings. How you relate to and respect
water is fundamental in creating living dynamic systems.

Mysteries of Water

Theoretical science has established patterns that most molecules follow, except the
water molecule. This abnormally small molecule should, according to the "rules of
the Periodic Table" turn from fluid to steam at – 75 C, but as we know, does this at
+ 100 C. According to the same Periodic Table, water should freeze at – 120 C but
of course does this at 0 C. And when it does freeze, it expands and floats in water!
No other substance does this.

Just think if water would had shrunk when frozen and sunk in water. Our world
would have been completely different from what it is today.

Water molecules form macro-molecules, called "clusters" in scientific language. These often form around other molecules such as proteins, acids, salts or sugars, creating the same shape as the encased molecule, but on a larger scale. When the encased molecule eventually filters out, the cluster of water molecules retains its shape, thus giving rise to the idea that water has memory. Even though the original molecule has gone, the shape of the cluster is still retained.

This may account for the subtle properties that water has when used as a homeopathic remedy. These remedies have been used for many generations by a great number of people, but are still under investigation, largely because they do not conform to the old hard science of the reductionist materialist paradigm.

Another strange fact is that about 70% of the surface area of our planet is covered by water, about the same percentage as we have water in our bodies. Is there a pattern here, or shall we hide behind the non-answer that it is mere coincidence? (Is calling things coincidences just another way of saying that we don't want to or can't be bothered to look for patterns?)

We can perceive clear patterns in the behaviour of water, even though hard science cannot explain why these patterns are as they are. As Permaculturalists we look for patterns where others don't perceive them.

☙❧

We are often told that water is life. Indeed, without water, life as we know it could not exist. We can't even survive for more than a few days without water, and we have probably all experienced a potted plant that we forgot to water, and came back to a week or two later to find dried out and dead.

In Permaculture design, water strategies are of crucial importance, and a great deal of planning goes into how we deal with too much water, too little water, and designing a balance between these two to give us a steady supply, for ourselves, for our plants and for our animals.

Some scientific research at the moment is aimed at finding out if the water on our planet is older than the sun, having been somehow locked up in minerals before the solar system assumed the shape that we know today. This is clearly pushing on the boundaries of the known and knowable, but might contain some interesting links with traditional creation stories.

In ChapterTwo, looking at soil and plants, we saw that there was a pattern corresponding between the blood in our bodies and the sap in plants. We might add to this also the role of water on our planet. The salt water in the oceans cycles around, evaporating to form clouds, falling as rain and running back into the ocean. This is an echo of the blood circulating in our bodies and the sap rising in plants.

"As above, so below" was the cry of the ancient alchemists and mystics. We may perceive the truth in this when we compare the patterns of sap, blood and water on our planet.

Characteristics of Water

Water can be regarded as being a border substance, a balancing substance. Its chemistry puts it exactly at the neutral point, balancing between acid and alkaline, and it can go either way. It might be regarded as an agent of chemical change.

It has no colour, it is neither dark nor light, and takes on whatever hue the surroundings might be. This will be obvious to anyone who has observed the ocean beneath different sky conditions. The deep blue of a cloudless summer day, the striking colours of a sunset reflected in the waves, or the ominous darkness of the sea under storm clouds.

The colours that we know appear clearly in the rainbow, another water phenomenon that is the source of many tales and legends.

Water is extremely heavy, as anyone who has carried buckets of water will confirm. However, if you immerse a heavy object in water, it will appear lighter, and ocean going ships weighing thousands of tons float easily on the surface of the sea, displacing a weight of water much greater than their own.

Ninty-seven per cent of the water on our planet is in the ocean, which covers 70 to 80 % of the Earth's surface.

It has been suggested that the stones of Stonehenge, one of the great stone monuments of Europe built many thousands of years ago, were floated from their original quarry in Wales, around the coast of Southern Britain and up the rivers to near the final resting place, so utilizing just this characteristic.

Water is often used by us as a means of storing and transporting heat. Water both radiates heat and conducts it. On the planet, enormous amounts of heat are transported across the oceans. The most well known is the Gulf Stream, carrying heat from the tropics around the Caribbean up to the far north of Arctic Norway and beyond. Similarly, cold is transported to warmer regions by ocean currents, for example, the Humboldt Current off the shore of Western South America creating fog far up the Chilean coast.

Theodor Schwenk comments that:

"In every area water assumes the role of mediator."

The shapes that water forms are some of the most basic and archetypal that we know. Placed on a horizontal surface a small drop of water will form a perfect circle, the drop. In motion, water will form spirals of various shapes and sizes, often complex and highly compounded. When the wind brushes across the surface of water, waves will form, and in the oceans, these can build up over considerable distances and when reaching a shelving shore, will break, forming tunnel-like rollers.

In addition to having such amazing qualities, if we look to water as we might to a teacher, it has messages that we would do well to listen to. Water is not rigid, and shapes itself to whatever surface presents itself.

This is something we might consider when confronted by new forms of thought. Do we reject them out of hand, or are we willing to take them into us, and work with them? Water seems the softest of substances, difficult to even grasp with a hand, but it wears away the hardest of substances, rock. Can we take hard thoughts and shape them to fit our own ideas?

The balancing qualities of water are also messages for us, if we are willing to listen. Can we create higher unities out of the polarities that confront us in life? When we discern the dualities of life and the cosmos, are we capable of finding the unity that lies within?

Water can be a great teacher, if we are willing to listen. Learning from nature is one of the central ideas in Permaculture.

Working with Water

For many years, inspired by the old mechanistic paradigm, it was fashionable to straighten rivers, to bury streams underground in pipes, and to drain swamps. All this in order to tidy up nature and to increase available farmland. This was done in good faith, often with only the best of intentions.

However, we now find that often this led to new problems that were not foreseen. In their lower reaches, rivers create meanders due to the tendency that water has to flow in curves. This makes the total length of the river longer, flattening out the gradient and slowing the flow. When the river is straightened, the flow rate increases and this sometimes causes flooding downstream. In the last few years, many European cities on the great rivers have experienced disastrous flooding.

On farmland the disappearance of streams, compounded by hedge clearance and tree felling, has led to a reduction in natural diversity and a consequent problem of pests and diseases in the crops being grown. The disappearance of large wetlands has also disrupted natural ecologies, in some cases changing bird migration patterns.

Nature has built up these complex systems in order to create diversity and so giving the environment a great deal of resilience. When we decrease variety, the ecosystem becomes fragile, and we experience increasing problems of pests, diseases and crop failures. As we learn to value the diversity, we are learning from nature, and

Bringing underground streams back onto the surface helps to improve diversity and vitality in the landscape.

the increasing interest in agro-forestry, forest gardens, conservation headlands and multi-cropping are all signs of progress in this direction. In all this, the behaviour of water is a key element of our design.

The recognition that water is much more than just a means of transport or a useful liquid is vital. As we delve deeper into water's characteristics, we rediscover that it has qualities that could be described as spiritual, that it is connected to the cosmos by such things as the ocean's tides, and that it is the great mediator in all things.

Flow Forms

As water flows, resistance is created between the water and the bed over which it flows. This in turn creates rhythms that sculpt the riverbed into often highly characteristic forms.

John Wilkes studied these forms as part of his training as a sculptor, and realized that he could create similar forms or bowls as "ready made" stream beds over which the water could be run. He called these bowls Flow Forms, and found that they influenced the water that passed across them.

They could be set up in series, creating a kind of stream or set of waterfalls. The forms induced the water to flow in a figure of eight pattern, known as a lemniscate, and these set up definite rhythms in the water. Different-shaped bowls created dif-

Flowform "Sevenfold", a great diversity of rhythms.

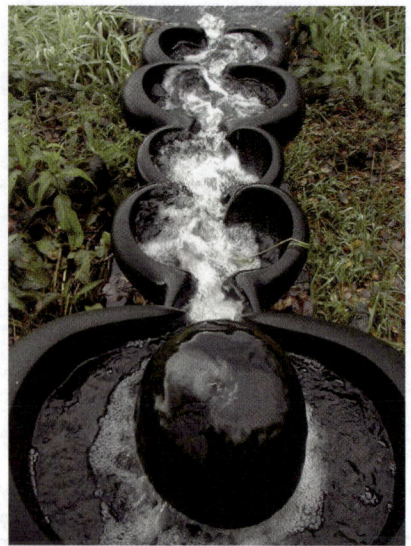

Flowforms used for wastewater treatment.

Flowform in Biodynamic herb garden, Camphill Copake, USA.

ferent rhythms, and the most complex of these he called the "Sevenfold" which has seven distinct bowls, each one different and creating a different rhythm.

By testing the water that had been passed over Flow Forms, Wilkes found that not only was the water oxygenated, it also was exposed to sunshine, and that it became "vitalized", being able to generate life in different ways.

Flow Forms have been used as a component in wastewater treatment, the increased vitality of the water encouraging the micro-organisms that break down the waste substances.

They have also been used as air conditioners in buildings, where the increased amounts of negatively charged ions have contributed positively to alleviate something often called the "sick building syndrome". Flow Forms are in demand for such places as doctor's surgeries, therapy clinics and large office complexes.

Measuring the Quality of Water

There are clear, hard science-type ways of measuring the quality of water. The most obvious are temperature, acidity, amount and type of suspended solids and various other fairly simple methods. Having been made aware of the myriad ways in which water may differ, we might look for more ways of measuring this.

How can we perceive differences in the water quality after it has passed through a series of Flow Forms, for example? For such subtle questions, hard science is not sensitive enough, and new ways of measuring quality have had to be developed. The researchers who have worked with Flow Forms have developed ways of checking how water responds to various treatments. The following are some of the repeatable methods that have been used for building up a picture of water's qualities:

Capillary dynamolysis

Ordinary filter paper is formed into a cylinder that is stood in a dish of the water to be tested. Capillary action pulls the liquid up into the paper, which is subsequently dried. The pattern on the filter paper can then be compared to other samples.

Chromatography

This is similar to the last system, except that here a horizontal disc of filter paper has the liquid drawn up into its centre, so that a series of concentric circles are formed as the liquid spreads out. Again, the disc is dried out and the results of a number of tests can be compared.

Crystallization

Copper chloride is added to the water samples to be tested. These samples are then allowed to dry out in an environment where the temperature and humidity are strictly controlled, to give every sample the same rate of evaporation. The resulting crystals from the various water samples can then be compared.

Drop picture Methods

In this case a fixed amount of glycerine is added to the samples to be tested, increasing their viscosity. The samples are then placed in a polished glass disc and distilled water is dropped from a constant height at a constant rate. The patterns that build up on the surface of each sample can be photographed and compared.

In all these methods an understanding of the different patterns created by different samples can be compared, and the observer has to build up a comparative analysis of the results. The picture that has emerged from the results of tens of thousands of these tests is that the purer the water, the more harmonic the pattern.

And conversely, the more the water has been polluted or contaminated by chemicals, the more chaotic the patterns. You can read more about these methods, and how they are used, in the book *Flowforms,* by John Wilkes.

There is another method of testing water, sometimes used in Permaculture courses. This consists of dividing the group into a number of smaller groups, each of which is given a jar, a dish, some absorbent paper and a handful of seeds, preferably wheat or lentils, that can be germinated.

The seeds are placed in dishes on absorbent paper and covered with a little cotton wool to reduce evaporation. Taking water from the same tap every day, each group undertakes to treat this water differently.

One group might add a controlled amount of liquid fertiliser. Another can spend ten minutes every day meditating on the water in silence. A third group can spend ten minutes shaking the jar rhythmically, with the lid on! A couple of groups do nothing to the water whatever. We call these the control groups.

You can make up more activities if there are more groups. The water is used to moisten the seeds twice daily for a week or 10 days, and then the sprouts of each group can be gently teased apart and put out on a piece of white paper, and the results compared.

This kind of exercise is good to start a discussion of water's qualities. Sometimes the results have been quite startling, but at other times we haven't experienced the great revelations that we might have expected. Clearly there are many more subtle things going on which are difficult to identify or control in a course situation!

Natural Wastewater Treatment at Findhorn

Natural wastewater treatment at Findhorn is based on a whole-systems approach to biological technology and utilizes a set of sequenced, complete ecologies. Tank-based systems treat sewage in a series of tanks. These tanks contain species that break down the sewage naturally.

In many systems, fish and plants are produced as by-products that can then be used or sold. This mirrors the process of decomposition that occurs in the natural world, but happens more intensively. At the end of the series of tanks, the resulting water is pure enough to re-use for non-potable applications or discharge directly to land, rivers or the ocean.

Natural treatment technologies are not only capable of meeting new, tough sewage outflow standards, but they also treat without the use of chemicals and are cost effective to re-use standards.

Treatment can be taken to advanced standards for water re-use in cost-effective projects, which are reliable, robust and aesthetically pleasing. This approach represents a shift from high energy, chemically intensive treatment to the adoption of the principles of ecological engineering.

Diverse communities of bacteria, algae, micro-organisms, numerous species of plants and trees, snails, fish and other living creatures interact as whole engineered ecologies in constructed wetlands, lagoons, tanks and biofilters, determined by the process design.

The Living Machine in the Findhorn Community.

Depending on the climate and the process, natural treatment systems can be located outdoors or in protective greenhouses.

The simplest and most cost-effective design consists of a septic tank and constructed wetland. This wetland has an impermeable liner, which isolates the treatment water from the groundwater. Wetland plants grow in gravel and the water flows horizontally through the gravel media and plant roots. This system is simple to construct and passive in its treatment except for pumping requirements.

However it requires the most land, of natural system designs. Systems that require less land are built in lagoons with floating ecologies or in tanks.

We have done considerable research into how water behaves, how we can manage it and how we use it in our towns, cities and in agriculture. We are not lacking in technical solutions to problems. But we are running out of clean, potable water. It seems that the solutions do not lie in the technical sphere, but somewhere else; how we think, how we feel and how we believe.

How can we create a consciousness about water that would lead us to bringing the solutions we already have to solving the challenges that confront us? Indeed, this is a serious question, because wars are already being fought partly fuelled by fears over water rights.

We have seen that water is the very stuff of life, and that we are seriously challenged in how we treat it today. We have also seen that solutions abound, and that many of them require a new relationship and a new appreciation of water.

Wetlands, Root Zone treatments, Living Machines and Flow Forms all represent various ways of approaching these solutions, and we suggest that these be made more well known, and that they be considered seriously by local authorities throughout the world.

We teach them in our Permaculture and Ecovillage courses.

Treating one's own waste is just the same as treating one's emotional, spiritual or mental body. All need to be cleaned and revitalized. It's a constant process, both within Nature and within people.

Findhorn is like a giant bioreactor with highly creative individuals, co-creating in a multitude of ways. And in the final analysis, water is akin to our emotions, and our emotions affect our interactions within all living systems.

The Living Machine is a place where one can meditate upon the evolutionary process of life. Life began in an anaerobic atmosphere and evolved through great waves of creation, each one giving birth to the next complexity. These waves of creation were usually preceded by a period of extinction, possibly to make space for newly evolving species.

As we embark on the next great wave of extinction, contemplating upon how water cleans itself deepens the meditative state and gives birth to solutions for a more sustainable future. (See introduction to Part Four – Bringing It All Together, page 149.)

CHAPTER FIVE

House Materials, Design and Building

To indigenous peoples, the whole land is home. The land is not merely property to be owned, but a spiritual landscape to be honoured in the image of the ancestors and heroes.
— DAVID PEARSON: *The Natural House Book.*

Land and People

The idea of "owning" your house or your land is something quite Western and fairly recent. We know that indigenous people, when asked by the first westerners about land ownership, replied that it was not a question of who owned the land, but the land that owned them.

Even today, among the landed aristocracy of Great Britain, there may well be a strong feeling that it is the responsibility of every generation to carry the ownership of the estates on to the next generation. Many of the landed gentry felt themselves "owned" by their estates.

The same feeling can be found amongst farmers where the farm has been in the same family for many generations. It may be easy to lose this feeling of responsibility when people move often, renting homes or farms, or buying and selling them on the open market; when property becomes something to trade in and speculate on.

Indeed, land speculation has drastically increased the price of land in some places to levels that make it totally unfeasible to create a surplus by farming it.

Communities, especially intentional communities such as Ecovillages, may be able to generate this attachment to the land and place, so that each individual feels a responsibility to the collective. One quite concrete way of generating this is to create quiet spaces for meditation, for prayer, for communing with nature spirits, or just to be quiet and appreciating the beauty and stillness of nature.

In his book *Timeless Way of Building*, published in 1979, Christopher Alexander writes about a nameless quality that pervades and informs all great building, both vernacular housing and monumental structures. This quality includes such aspects as vitality, wholeness, comfort, freedom, eternity and lack of ego.

This quality has to do with our own feeling of well-being, our good health,

A tipi points up at the sky and the heavens, reminding us of deep cosmic connections.

and it could be summed up in the word "alive", as in the sense of something being alive. We know intuitively what it means to be alive, but for sure, each one of us would probably define it differently. This is the nameless quality that Christopher Alexander is referring to.

In a subsequent book, *Pattern Language*, he goes on to break up the designing process into 247 "Patterns", and puts them in a sequence that echoes the Permaculture principle of designing from patterns to details.

The first Pattern is bioregional, the last describes the shelf next to the front door. The book does not have to be read in a strict order, however, each design can be built up using a different set of Patterns. The principle of designing from patterns to details is kept throughout by references at the beginning of each Pattern referring to relevant Patterns that might be useful background, and at the end of each Pattern referring to possible follow ups for more detail.

This book, *Pattern Language*, is highly recommended as a manual for any Permaculture designer. One Ecovillage group in Britain in the 1970s made reading it a requirement of membership.

One of the aspects of this "nameless quality" that Alexander writes about is the impossibility of pinning it down to a word or a description. It really is nameless, but it is recognizable to those who understand it. In a way, it crosses over to the spiritual dimension.

If you don't know what we are writing about, there is nothing we can do to convince you otherwise, but as soon as it's recognized, there is mutual understanding. It may indeed be easier to find it by example rather than trying for abstract definitions.

If you are walking in a natural area, a beach, a forest, or up on the moors, try to be aware of where you would like to take a rest. What place invites you to sit down and relax your legs? What place has a good view of either where you walked, or the area where you are heading? Why do you choose this place, and not another? The answers to these questions will help you to define what this nameless quality might be.

Many people agree that a Greek village, with its whitewashed square buildings cut through by narrow stepped alleyways, is a marvellous place to visit and stay in. Or an Italian hilltop village, low stone houses with pantiled red roofs. Traditional vernacular housing, however, is limited to local materials and traditions that have not changed for centuries, sometimes millennia.

Today, the economics of building and the wealth of the western world have freed us from all limitations, and rich western people build their villas in whatever style they like. We always thought that freedom is a good and positive thing, except when confronted by modern suburban housing, and the realization that total freedom of style leads to complete chaos and lack of any unifying features.

There's really nothing worse and more disturbing than many of today's up-market housing developments, where each family home is trying to outdo all the others in extravagances.

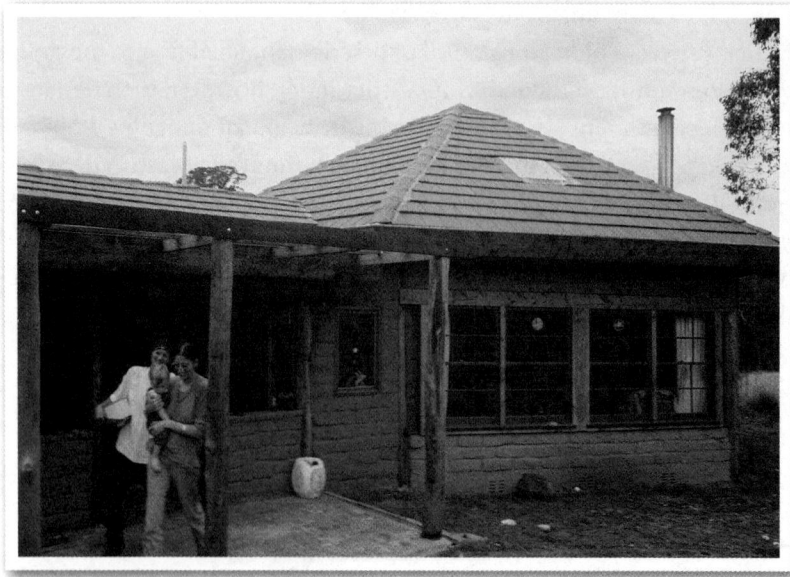

Mud brick house at Sunrise Farm community in Australia.

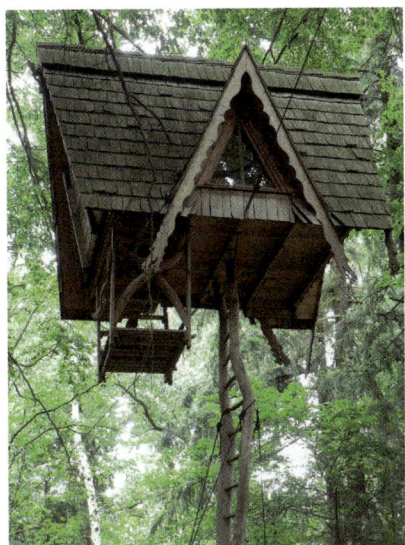

Tree house near ZEGG Ecovillage in Germany .

Traditional Italian village roofs.

It may have something to do with the process. In most modern building, the emphasis is on the product, the house or the building, which is drawn, often repeatedly, in more and more detail by the architect or designer. (This is actually what we teach in Permaculture, and our Design Courses always end with the presentations by the participants of really good designs that they have been working on throughout the course, often buildings.)

In the western world it has become the norm to take the building design, run it by a number of builders, and choose either the cheapest, or the one we like the best. Then they build. Exactly what we designed.

This is not the way most traditional, vernacular buildings used to be constructed, and certainly not the way those charming Greek and Italian villages were built. Usually there was no drawing, no design, no architects, and no professional builders. The community would get together, the only materials were those to hand in the local ecology, and the only designs were the ones that had been used for generations which everyone knew because that's where they lived.

Any specialized builders would have learnt from other specialized builders, traditions handed down from master to apprentice.

Occasionally these traditional ways of building are encapsulated on film, and anyone who has seen *Witness*, a film from the 1970s set in the Amish community of the USA, or *The True Dirt on Farmer John*, a film from 2003 about farming in the USA, will remember the barn-raising scenes.

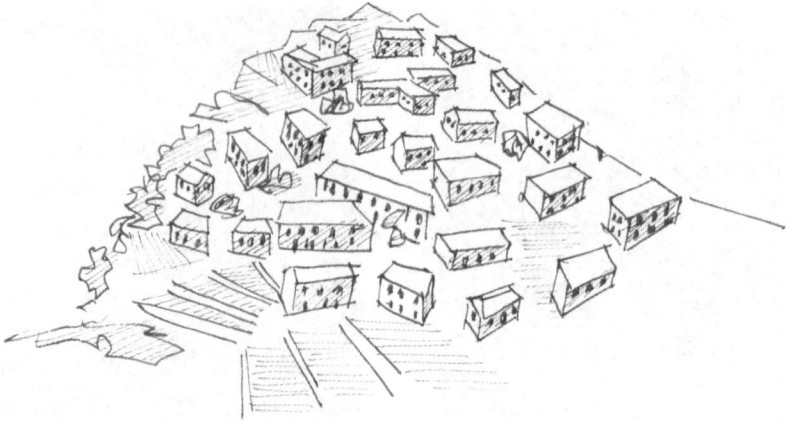

Traditional Italian village design.

Some Ecovillages have gone down this road, at least for a time, by working to-gether to build their houses, often out of local materials such as straw bales, earth or timber. However, the twin nightmares of planning regulations and financing have forced most western Ecovillages to build with designs drawn by certified architects and builders using modern industrial materials, and the actual work carried out by contracted entrepreneurs hiring outside labour.

We may be asking ourselves if this impacts upon the spiritual quality of the building itself.

Can we design a way of listening to the location, listening to which materials present themselves in the locality, and to the people, the community that is going to live and work in these buildings? How do we listen? How can we develop a culture of dialogue with these elements?

Again, we can use the Permaculture principle of asking questions rather than trying to answer them for others. Each person, each family and each community would answer these questions in different ways, and may indeed go on to ask a dif-ferent set of questions, and come to different solutions.

Indigenous Habitat

One way of creating a dialogue with the locality is to look at the original indigenous buildings and study the methods and materials used. These buildings developed with an intimate knowledge of the local environment and conditions, and often contain much wisdom which modern architects and builders have possibly over-looked or missed.

If no original buildings exist, look at the history of the original people and how and where they lived. You might want to ask what they were made of and where they were built, and how they evolved into the present day structures. Don't just research human dwellings, include other buildings of many categories; sacred and profane, temples, shrines, barns, mills, storage houses and out-houses.

What are the passive features, using the four elements of Earth, Air, Fire, and Water? How were local resources maintained or were they finally exhausted?

We might look closer at what kind of materials were used, and divide them up into earth-based, plant-based and animal-based. A question we might ask ourselves here is if these materials have any kind of deeper or spiritual value. Alanna Moore writes in her book *Sensitive Permaculture* that the "*...soul-stuff of a house is said to accumulate through the choice of materials...*"

Earth-based materials can be divided into a range of sizes, the largest size being stones, the smallest mud or clay, which is composed of microscopic pieces of stone held together in a matrix of moisture and electrical impulses called ions, forming colloids.

Some people experience earth-based materials, especially clay, as having a heaviness that can be oppressive. Others experience clay and mud as highly plastic and capable of being sculpted into weaving and soaring forms. Clay-based buildings are perhaps the most widespread of the traditional building types in the world.

Traditional Mongolian yurt, or "Ger" in ZEGG Ecovillage, Germany.

Traditional Norwegian Stave church: sacred architecture grounded
in the ecology of Scandinavia.

We like to think of earth-based materials as taking us back to the cave dwellers. The thermal mass of caves helps to even the temperature, making it relatively cool in a hot summer, and warm during the harsh cold of the winter. But caves are of essence immovable, so forcing the dweller to stay in one place. Houses built of stone and brick fall into this category.

The other category of shelter that was used by the first human groups was based on plant materials, rushes, grasses, branches and leaves, in some cases augmented by animal skins. These are highly mobile, easy to erect, take down and even move from place to place. But of course they don't protect so much from the elements,

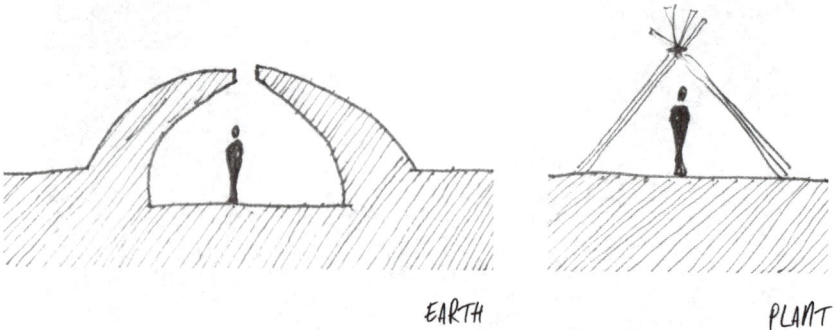

EARTH   PLANT

Two categories of shelter: building based on earth, building based on plants.

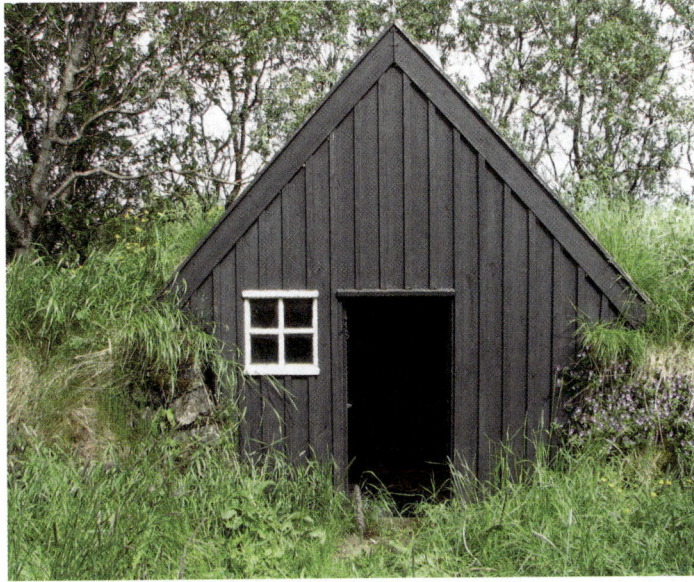

Sod and stone foundation house in Iceland.

and are subject to the changes in temperature and precipitation. Tipis and yurts, the mudhifs of Iraq, and the lavvo of the Samis fall into this category.

In our list of materials we must not forget animal-based shelters such as yurts, or gerts, covered with wool-based felt, or the indigenous American tipi, covered in buffalo hides. In addition, sinews have been used to tie, weave or hold things together. Do these bring with them some of the qualities of the animals from where they came?

Whatever values we give to different materials, it's clear that by giving them such values, we invest the structure with qualities that are beyond the merely material. We come back to that subtle feeling of a place or a building having that feeling of "being right".

It's hard to define in material terms, but many of us recognize it when we meet it. We can cultivate it by practising peaceful contemplation, and by arranging materials, pictures and objects in various ways. Alanna Moore suggests:

"…we can raise positive energy and give thanks for what we have been given so generously…"

Mud house in Israel, inspired by traditional Rajasthani building techniques and styles, note the overhang to protect the walls.

We have already seen how plants may be seen to be imbued with different spiritual values, and extending this to the materials used in a building, ask ourselves if there is a qualitative difference between a house built of birch or willow, from one built of oak. There are many other plant-based materials that have been in use.

The sod houses of Iceland and the west coast of Northern Europe, the mudhifs that were in use in Mesopotamia for millennia, in Iraq, as recent as just a generation ago. The modern version is straw bale housing, an iconic feature of many Permaculture-inspired Ecovillages.

In our modern, post-industrial and highly ecological culture we have been experimenting with recycled materials. The Earthships developed by Mike Reynolds use old tyres, plastic and glass bottles and even old beer and soft drinks cans as basic building blocks. Do they bring with them any specific spiritual qualities? What happens to these over the life cycle of the building? Do they sink back onto the ground after the building has finished its life, to become a pile of garbage in the desert?

We are great admirers of the Earthship experiment, but have heard people having misgivings about what happens in the long run. But maybe even a small pile of garbage gradually sinking back into the earth is preferable to the enormity of the landfills they would otherwise contribute to. Nothing is perfect, everything has its price, what is appropriate in one place may not be so in another.

It is ironic and reassuring that the less affluent nations are often producing more ecological and sometimes the most beautiful buildings. Somehow, by having lim-

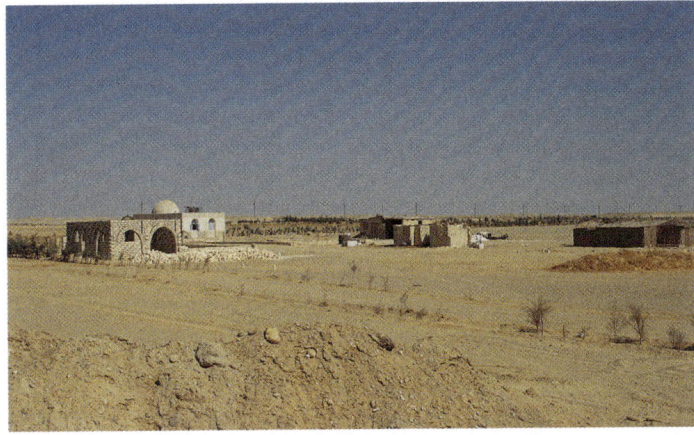

New Bassaisa Ecovillage in Egypt, using local sand,
clay and rock for building.

ited technical and economic resources, practical intelligence is directed towards creative and imaginative responses to meeting our human needs within nature and the environment. We use the materials nature has provided for us in the immediate context in the most natural and affordable state.

Such intelligence can be an inspiration to us all if we make an effort to reduce over-manipulation of natural resources and question the reasons we do this.

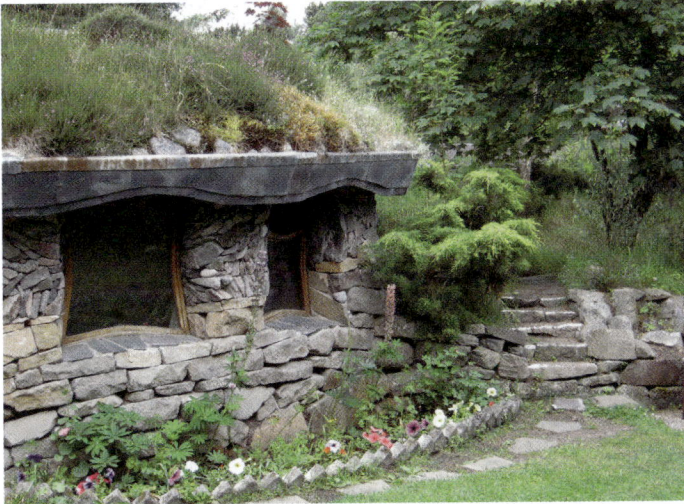

Findhorn Nature Sanctuary, hand-built with stones from a nearby quarry
and reclaimed local materials.

Natural and Low-Tech Houses at Findhorn

Findhorn has numerous examples of ecological housing strategies such as living roofs, breathing walls, passive and active houses and reuse of local materials.

One of the Findhorn Foundation's most important elements of planning involves tuning into our innate wisdom when considering a new building project. We employ a combination of gathering knowledge and information about the project and then endeavour to also consider the "bigger picture" of things. Honouring the spirit of nature, tuning into what is right on all levels; our needs, nature's needs and the needs of future generations.

This is the process of "attunement" and it usually involves taking some quiet time in the midst of discussion and information sharing. We always try to do this outside on the land where the project is proposed in order to get a sense of the context.

This way we have the opportunity to visualize it there and then, and feel into the spirit of the land and see if it feels right. This is not always an easy thing to do. You could call it working with mind and heart. The process of becoming one with "all-at-one-with".

Lyle Schnadt wrote in *Faces of Findhorn* in 1980 that:

> *"To me it would be ridiculous to hire a regular construction company with aggressive or hostile interrelationships to, say, build a church. You could do it, but you'd just end up with a mere building; whereas, if you have people who are discovering who God is in the process of building, then you have a much more profound space in which to come together as a congregation.*
>
> *In the same way, I feel it's important for families to build their own homes and thereby discover more about how to work together. Then their home actually supports them in being a family."*

Lyle's dream is Craig's dream and he has done exactly that, building a home and raising a family in Findhorn. But pioneers such as Craig are challenged by the majority of people wanting something similar but not having the skill or the time to do so. They need it to be done for them and it's then that the paradigm changes.

Architects, engineers, building regulations and planning authorities all co-opt those ideas and integrate them into modern co-housing eco-settlements. They become more commercial, speculative and expensive. As the dream matures the challenge becomes to infuse it with the same spirit from which it was born.

Low-tech houses in the Findhorn Community.

Once we have built the perfect sustainable dwelling we fill it with light, and see it in context; in Zone 1 in Permaculture language. Surrounded by its gardens in Zone 2, then larger scale food production in Zone 3, edible landscapes and woodlands in Zone 4 and on out to the wilderness of sand dunes and sea in Zone 5.

All this integrated into the bioregion of Forres. At Findhorn we add Zones 0 and 00, 0 being the relationships between those living in the settlement and 00 your own personal soul journey, that inner core connecting you with all life.

You stand back and see a Permaculture settlement in its full featured-ness. Windmills whirl above roof tops shining with solar collectors, there are shops, cafés, meditation spaces, gardens and woodlands; a laboratory for exploring the next frontiers of humanity's evolutionary relationship with the living intelligence of this planet.

Bill Mollison was inspired by the wisdom within a rainforest and traditional villages around the world that have lived in balance with nature. He was also inspired by the Tao, a holistic view based on the interaction of living things and their dependence upon each other.

Findhorn is inspired by that same interaction. We are like peas in a pod, each one unique, nurtured by the unpredictable patterns of nature that allow for development and change.

Environmental Standards
at Findhorn Ecovillage

At Findhorn new environmental products are continually being developed and tested, as well as those that claim to be green but aren't. We use a number of criteria in evaluating products and techniques. The basic line is that they have to be non-toxic, natural and with a low embodied energy.

We take into consideration the affordability of the product and its life-cycle cost. We like our products to be friendly to the installer, the user and to the Earth, with a maximum recycling potential. We look into conserving water, resources and energy, and we like our products to be local and renewable if possible. We are aware of radon protection, and take that into account on our building sites.

These criteria are not fixed and there is a need for conscious decision-making where compromises are thought necessary. Flexibility is another important quality that we look for, something that is reflected in the Permaculture principle of being pragmatic rather than dogmatic. Permaculture builders make do with what they have.

We have built up quite a body of expertise and are happy to share this within the community as well as with other groups and organizations to increase our knowledge and stay current and informed. Networking with environmental builders and designers is an important part of our work, a way of creating a wider dissemination of ecological building.

Universal Hall as Sacred Geometry

The Universal Hall at Findhorn is both sacred and profane, designed to be a multi-functional building serving the many needs of a growing spiritual community. Intuitively designed and constructed, concretized with solid skill and labour. Neither flashy nor gilded, yet powerfully present, this unusual five-sided building embodies an innate wisdom within its bones and spirit.

There is much that can be said about the sacred geometry of its design. The most obviously striking feature is that it has five sides, a Pentagon in geometrical terms. The number five is said to represent the perfection of humanity, the meeting of spirit and form, and arising from the Pentagon we get a five-pointed star, a Pentagram.

This illustrates the perfect full circle of humanity through incarnation, and a return to the One by a path of involution and evolution. It shows involution into matter, evolution of matter to human form, and the horizontal process of incarnation that demonstrates that humanity makes no progress on its own.

Universal Hall

Flow creativity art

It is important to emphasize that most of these characteristics evolved through an intuitively guided plan rather than through conscious intention. The hall is one of the most important structures in the community as it provides the space for us to explore and synthesize our collective intentions, and when that becomes too serious, a place to sing and dance and just have fun.

We like to make the analogy of it being like a greenhouse in the garden where you can warm things up and hasten their growth before planting them out, but in the Universal Hall we're not growing plants, we are growing people.

We are growing community.

Building Me Wee House

IN 1981, I WAS ASKED by then Foundation focaliser Francois Duquesne to organize a conference called Building a Planetary Village. Why "Planetary"? Because Findhorn was meant to be a place that took the planet as a whole, as our primary address and context. And because it was increasingly populated by people from all over the world.

Anyway, the conference was meant to "set the scene" and present the vision for the purchase of the caravan park that had been the original home of the Foundation community. Management was then poised to embark on its purchase, despite having precious little cash in the kitty.

By way of conference preparation, we invited two architects from California, Sim van der Ryn and James Hubbell, to come over and do some design "charettes" with us. Not surprisingly, when community members began to dream into the prospect of actually owning the Park and commence permanent building here, lots of circles and spirals became apparent, probably as a reaction to living for years in the tin boxes we call "caravans".

In any case, the conference came and went in October 1982, leaving an exquisite flurry of grand visions and designs in its wake.

The following year, 1983, saw the purchase of the caravan park, made possible largely by myriad small donations by thousands of Foundation supporters from around the world who wanted to see our visions become "manifestations".

In October 1984 I returned from a sabbatical year in California, only to discover that NOT a great deal had happened towards actually building the planetary village, mainly because the Foundation was still absorbed by cash flow issues and "capital" was nowhere to behold.

In January 1985, I paid a visit to nearby Speyside Cooperage to collect some free firewood in the form of old barrel staves. I was also shown six large "marrying vessels" they had recently removed from a distillery in Fife and they asked if I had any interest in them. I initially declined, but then discovered that the vessels began "speaking" to me in the form of suggesting various possible applications in the community.

As we were then contemplating a Community Centre Extension and starting a Steiner School, I reckoned these beautiful vessels could well come in handy. All my suggestions were nixed, mainly because the wood was suffused with "spirits".

It became apparent that if anyone was going to use these vessels, it would have to be me.

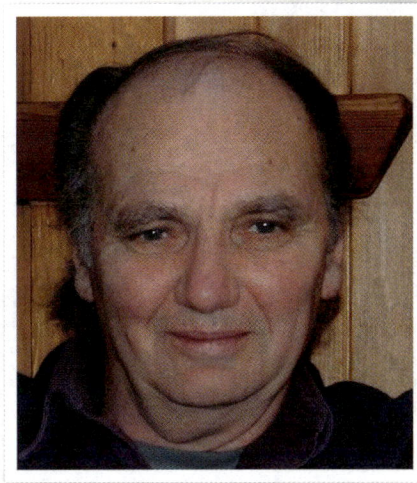

Roger Doudna

I broke ground in March 1985 and was accorded the free assistance of both Keith Wilcox (community gardener and architect) and Andy Shorrock (resident builder) for three months by the Foundation. After that, I was largely on my own, though the Foundation eventually accorded the project sufficient credibility to allow those guests, who were game, to help me as part of the official guest programme.

I would also relentlessly consult competent community builders on the countless "challenges" encountered along the way. It took a year to complete the barrel itself, and another three months to do the conservatory extension. I remember the building process as long and exhausting, but it was also continually inspiring as well.

I would never have made it without all the assistance the community provided, including access to its tools, facilities, guests and expertise. It cost about £10,000 both to build and furnish with bits and bobs that I mostly bought at local auctions.

Though the project elicited lots of media interest throughout, it was kind of "crowned" by a feature Christmas piece that appeared in virtually every newspaper in the land and beyond.

I returned from my Christmas holiday in the USA to see my house in everything from the tabloids to the broadsheets with memorable headings like "Daffy Doc Lives in a Vat", "Vat's Life!" "Life's a Dram", etc. Even the TV crowd was after me. So, I had my 15 minutes of fame and that was nice enough.

What did I learn from this experience? For one thing, ideas and "visions" are a dime a dozen. Putting them into action can easily take all you got on all levels. But what else are we here for? Peter Caddy, Findhorn founder, managed to reduce his community 'lessons' to nice wee sayings like "work is love in action".

Roger Doudna's Whiskey Barrel House.

One of his favourite 'recipes' for creating the community was 'the 3 Ps – patience, persistence and perseverance'. I certainly learned that one. And indeed the other one as well. *I built this house because I knew I could, and I wanted to do it for and with the community I love.* My greatest ordeal was securing its consensual support, but once I had it, the rest flowed beautifully, if demandingly. I really did love the building bit, because I proved to myself I could do something of consequence that I had never done before.

Hence the experience qualifies in my mind as a bona fide 'initiation' into the wonders of what's possible when you put your mind, heart and will into it. Not unlike Findhorn itself in that respect.

Most of all, I love what's happened since. 'Me wee house' seems to have helped unblock the log jam of doubt and fear around what we can do with this place and literally opened the floodgates to the possibility of building a sustainable planetary (oops) ECO-village right here and now. And 30 years later we're well on our way.

And now that 'sustainability' itself is widely perceived as humanity's 'final frontier', it seems we're 'ahead of the game' in terms of pioneering a more viable and harmonious lifestyle for others as well.

NOTE: *Roger Doudna, philosopher, Whisky Barrel House builder arrived in Findhorn in 1974. Inspired by Spiritual Teacher, David Spangler's description of the community as a place of vision and transformation he set about developing international conferences that would reflect that aspect.*

A doyen of the community, Roger created and organizes the world-wide Findhorn Fellows Association.

CHAPTER SIX

Energy Sources and Alternative Technology

*I know your every need, and your every need is being
wonderfully met. Believe it with all your heart.
Never at any time allow a single doubt in to
mar the wonder of it. Accept My word, live by it,
and see miracle upon miracle take place.
The time of miracles is certainly not over.*

— *EILEEN CADDY.*

*"At the cutting edge of science today, a powerful new awakening
is taking place in many different disciplines. The key insight is
this: beyond the physical realm, there exist invisible patterns and
principles that somehow organize what we observe and experience in the physical world. Science is discovering that 'something
transpires behind that which appears'."*

— *WILL KEEPIN, The Song of the Earth.*

Spaceship Earth

*"We are travelling at enormous speed through uncharted territory. Our
ship is one of a kind, almost perfectly round and coloured a lovely blue.
Although quite old now, she comes from a time when things were designed
to last and from a place where it was assumed that the crew and passengers would work together for the benefit of all.*

*She is equipped with a revolutionary outer shield, capable of simulta-
neously protecting her passengers, whilst admitting the energy required,
keeping the whole system going. Within the shield the ship maintains a
comfortable internal environment to suit the myriad species that are her
passengers. It has been a long journey and many, many generations have
lived safely in her care."*

— *Applied Ecovillage Course Manual, Findhorn.*

Recognize the ship? This is where we live – our beautiful planet Earth. Not so long ago it seems that our ship was indestructible. But we are slowly becoming aware that the actions of a number of the passengers are putting the lives of all the passengers at risk. Talk of complete catastrophe no longer seems like idle speculation. There is the distinct possibility that the entire ship will founder and sink.

The Foundations of Technology in Science

As we saw in the opening chapter, advances in science are showing us that a new way of seeing the world is emerging. This can be summed up as the realization that there is a spiritual dimension behind or beyond the physical one.

That this is happening in the hard sciences, and across the scientific field, from biology and physics to psychology and physiology, is confirming insights from mystics throughout the ages.

After three centuries during which science and spirituality have been moving further apart we are now entering an era where the two have the possibility of forming a "seamless unity" as Will Keepin calls it.

This realm of spirit in science has been identified by physicist David Böhm as the "implicate order". It's not just a vague addendum to the physical world that we all know and acknowledge, but is the fundamental reality, the origin and source of the physical world as we know it. This is how the findings of the new paradigm in cutting edge science is turning the world, as we know it, upside down.

When we come to consider energy and technology, we need to consider these things as the manifestations of energy or spirit in the physical world.

To sum up, the spiritual dimension is the basic creation, and the material world is founded upon that dimension.

Patterns in Nature

Geometry is one of the foundations of the physical universe, and from this Permaculture has taken the study and use of patterns as one of its basic principles. This is an area where the physical and the organic overlap, and we find patterns that replicate in both minerals and in live organisms.

Even though the universe in all its glory seems apparently varied, there are actually just a few patterns that are endlessly repeated in both size and combination. Fractals are perhaps one of the best known of these in modern science, and though amazingly complex, they actually just repeat a basic formula in ever increasing or diminishing size.

THE WAVE

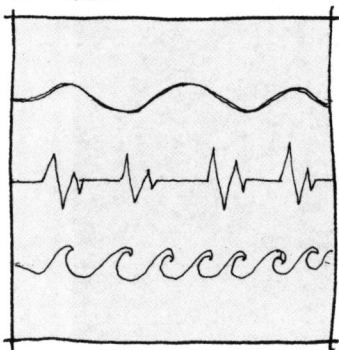

THE LOBE

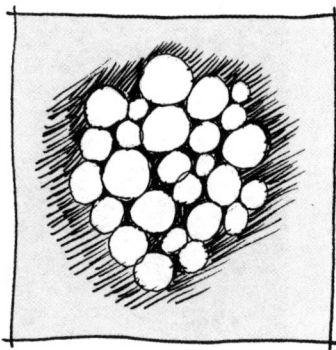

THE SPIRAL

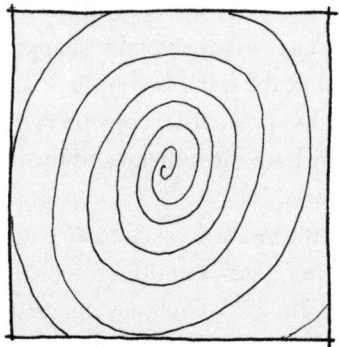

THE NET

THE SCATTER

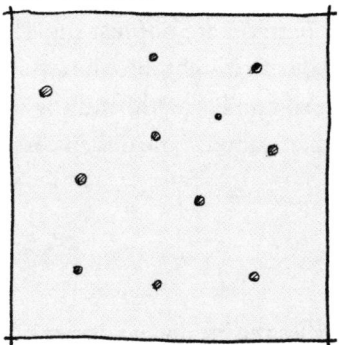

THE BRANCH

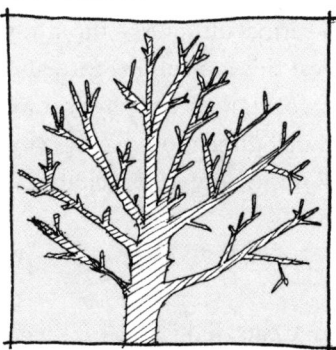

Examples of patterns in nature.

Intricate patterns on tree bark.

The spiral is another of these basic patterns that seem to be repeated in unlimited variations. Sea creatures construct shells that have many different shapes and sizes. These shells are usually of chalk, a mineral, but the spiral is also the shape of DNA, which is now being charted as the information packet that constructs living creatures, including us. The spiral is a form used by both the mineral and the plant and animal world.

Spiritual paths across the world and throughout time have taken basic patterns as their symbols. Sacred geometry can be found in religious buildings, churches, temples, shrines and monasteries in all religions. The cross, the star, the crescent (moon) and the twin spirals of the yin/yang symbol are just a few of the best known.

The geometry used in sacred structures are as old as human culture, indeed, it may be argued that these patterns are as old as consciousness itself.

To Permaculturalists, the study of these basic patterns are not just superficial technical aids to planning gardens, walls or paths, but an insight into the structure of the world, both the physical world that we are so familiar with, and the other world, that dimension that has emerged in all human cultures, the dimension that we call spirituality or consciousness.

Questioning

Callum Coats, in his book *Living Energies* chronicles the life and achievements of Viktor Schauberger, who began by looking at how water behaved, and gradually got into all kinds of research on energy and energy production in such fields as: implosion rather then explosion; biological vacuums; Repulsators and Klimators.

A controversial figure working at the boundaries of science, and often vilified by his scientific and technical contemporaries, Schauberger posed a great number of questions, which is maybe the best way to approach science and technology. As we have seen in Permaculture, it is framing the right questions that starts us on a road to design that may be most fruitful. Here are some of the questions Schauberger asked:

- Why does the Earth rotate from west to east?
- Why do gases condense with a decrease in temperature?
- Why doesn't the Earth's warm air rise?
- Why is it so cold at the top of a mountain, ie., nearer the sun?
- Why do damp tiled roofs dry out from the eaves towards the ridge?
- Why do west-to-east flowing watercourses fertilize their banks?
- Why are the banks of east-to-west flowing rivers so barren?
- Why does a trout stand still in a raging torrent, as if by magic?

These questions often reveal intense and detailed observation, and lead us to wonder at the laws and rules that govern nature. To say "I don't know", or "it's just a coincidence" is not good enough, we need to look deeper into our world, and realize that technology and science as they are today have barely scratched the surface of the world.

There is so much that we don't know, that to dismiss any question as useless or any new insights as irrelevant is actually unscientific, and not worthy of the spirit of enquiry that has led leading scientists throughout the ages to deepen our knowledge of the world.

Permaculture needs to develop just this spirit of enquiry, to ask questions about the world and to try to find answers to them. Science and technology are fields of enquiry that give us the opportunity to relate to the world we find ourselves in, to provide us with the tools we need to create the world we want.

Energy, food, housing, clothing, communication and the documentation and storage of knowledge are all things that we need to cultivate, and without technology these things cannot be done.

Energy Context Today

Arguably the most important environmental aspect of building when looking at the world situation is the use of energy. Currently 20% of the world's population uses 80% of the available energy and most of those live in the western industrialized nations.

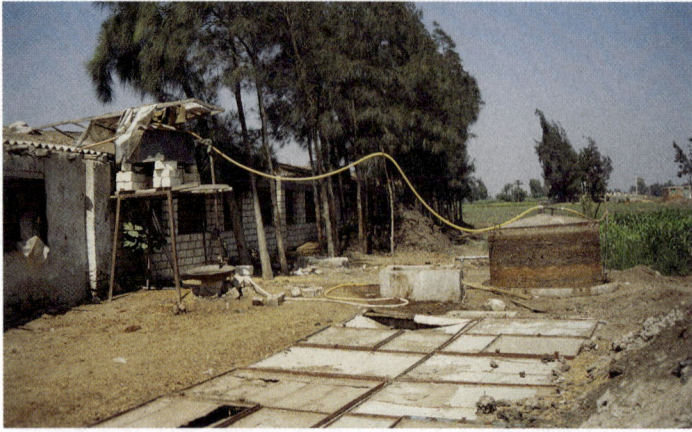

Methane gas generated from animal and human waste, Nile Delta, Egypt.

Most of the world's pollution is caused by the consumption of that energy and the related industrial processes that have grown out of this same society. We have based our society on an artificially low and quite unreal price for energy, especially oil and coal. None of the environmental costs resulting from their use are factored in, or have even been considered until recently.

Most of the energy sources we currently use, ie., coal, oil and gas, are non-renewable and limited in supply. Yet we continue to use them in ever-increasing amounts.

The advances in technology of all kinds have, to a large degree, been beneficial and eliminated much human suffering. But our blindness to the many side effects caused by our consumption of energy has led us to become wasteful and careless of these valuable resources. Clearly, if the standard of living of the rest of the world is to be brought up to that of the West, the same technologies cannot be applied without massive environmental degradation and destruction.

In temperate and cold climates human beings need to have heat for their homes and a large portion of the energy consumed in our dwellings is used to provide it. We also need energy in the home for lighting and appliances and for hot water for washing and bathing.

The only long-term strategy for getting a handle on our energy consumption is to build our homes and other buildings so that they use as little energy as is necessary to provide for our basic needs.

The same human intelligence that has transformed the world over the past century and developed instant world-wide communication networks, space travel and the inner workings of a nuclear power station can certainly overcome the technical problems associated with insulating buildings and using energy efficiently.

Renewable Energy at Findhorn

We need to address both the energy conservation question and the energy source issue. For along with the minimizing of our need for energy we need to develop clean and renewable sources to meet our needs, rather than relying on the diminishing and polluting alternatives. Renewable energy and energy conservation go hand in hand.

As part of a sustainable lifestyle, we are committed to the long-term use of benign and renewable energy sources and systems. In the Moray Firth, Scotland, region wind energy combined with passive and active solar systems in new buildings form a viable energy alternative to the conventional highly polluting, inefficient and non-renewable fossil fuel and nuclear energy options.

At Findhorn we have chosen to adopt our own energy conservation standards, which are approximately 2.5 times better than the normal Scottish standards. After several years at this level we feel we could still do better.

For all that we have done at Findhorn with renewable energy the paradigm keeps changing. With Peak Oil and more innovative renewable technologies emerging there is an opportunity for us to begin the next generation of renewable energy development.

Our greatest challenge is to not just sit back on what we have achieved but stay engaged with the latest innovations and use our community as a testing ground. It's just like any spiritual practice; you need to practice daily always renewing yourself, staying open to feedback, letting go of old patterns and allow energy to flow and, wherever possible, keep it simple.

Wind power has tremendous possibilities as a source of energy.

Sustainability is a key element of the vision for the Findhorn Foundation Community Ecovillage. Environmental sustainability means not using resources faster than the Earth can create them and not emitting wastes faster than the Earth can absorb them. *This is critical*. Social and economic sustainability are equally critical.

The Findhorn Foundation Community is an on-going, evolving demonstration of how humans can live in co-operation with the natural environment, rather than exploiting and depleting it, in a way that supports the fullest development of individuals, society and commerce.

Peak Oil and Climate Chaos

We have known for a long time that oil is a non-renewable resource, but it is only in the last decade that some people have begun to take the issue seriously. Basically it would seem that oil extraction takes the pattern of a bell curve, whether it's applied to a single oil well, an oil field, or the world's oil extraction as a whole. The bell curve is symmetrical, so the second, declining half is roughly a mirror image of the first, ascending half.

We started using oil on an industrial scale at the beginning of the 20th Century, and have now reached the top of the curve, meaning that a hundred years from now there will be only negligible amounts of oil being pumped out of the ground.

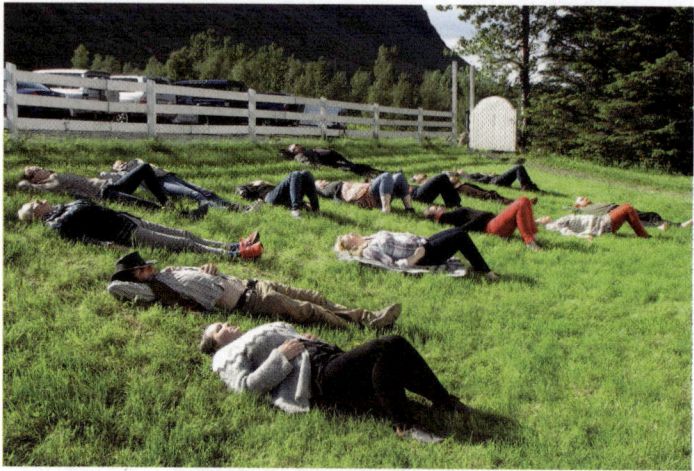

Icelandic students of Permaculture Design, enjoying the free benefits of solar energy.

Because our civilization is massively founded on oil in all its uses, we clearly need to develop a technology that is less dependent upon oil. There's no need to panic, we have a century to do so, but not to address the situation at all is obviously going to lead to chaos and trouble when oil begins to become scarcer and more expensive. This is something we will begin to experience in the next few decades.

The profligate use of oil as our right and fighting wars with other nations in order to control the sources of our oil is a loser's strategy. There is enough for everyone's need, but not for everyone's greed. If we could use the resources at our disposal to find alternatives to oil, we could save ourselves a lot of trouble and a great deal of human tragedy.

Most scientists who have researched the changing climate on our planet over the last decades have reached a common conclusion that our technology is contributing to climate change. This is usually referred to as "global warming" or "climate change" but our experience of this is more in the realm of increasingly chaotic and unpredictable weather conditions. Whatever we call it, there are solutions to be found in our technologies, and these are neither very expensive, nor very complicated.

Indeed, most of them are already right there under our noses, and just need to be developed. In energy we have solar, wind and wave waiting to be harnessed, and indeed they are already becoming an increasing factor. In materials use we have many alternatives to oil-based technologies. In agriculture, organic farming is viable, increasing and has even been shown to be healthier than industrial/chemical agribusiness: a real free side effect!

For carbon capture we have tree planting, something most people can engage in.

All the solutions, all the answers, they are right there. *They don't need to be invented.* Their application is not a technical issue, but is based on a new consciousness.

Compassion is a solution to all our problems. Compassion for the planet and all who travel on her is a way of entering the new spiritualty that we need to rescue the ship we call Earth.

Permaculture:
A Spiritual Approach

MY REAL AWAKENING came outdoors in the wilds of the Pacific Northwest, the Cascade Mountains of Oregon state. With a very urban upbringing I first found my connection with the natural world at about the age of 12 on a blue sky day overlooking a snowy world and a towering mountain.

Through my teen years, being on that mountain or on the trails and forests around her, that relationship grew; the beauty and awe-inspiring perfection of Nature stirring something deep inside that eventually lead me to the famous gardens of Findhorn in my mid-20s.

I had studied engineering at university, mostly due to parental pressure and the fear of not being employable, and then worked a few years in a huge steel fabrication factory, just long enough to finish my professional qualification. And long enough to realize that this was not what I wanted to do for the rest of my life. Now at Findhorn I imagined leaving all that behind and working as a gardener. But it wasn't long before I was "asked" to help in the maintenance and building department. So much for being a gardener! During that first year the early ideas for ecovillages emerged: villages that reflected a deep connection to the land and culture in which they were based, but that also held a planetary and spiritual consciousness/awareness.

John Talbott

This caught my attention and for the first time I saw how a technical background might be used in a way that was meaningful and connected to a deep relationship to Nature.

This call was so strong – I can remember the first writing I did for Findhorn on our "land ethic"– I got a sense of Nature speaking through me. We humans needed to find a kinder, less destructive way to live on the Earth, and Nature wanted to co-create and work with us. Maybe we could even reshape our settlements to be life enhancing, not just for humans but for all life. What a thought!

I spent the next 24 years helping to ground that vision at Findhorn and on the way helped to set up the Global Ecovillage Network, discovered Permaculture, and many other impulses guiding us towards life-enhancing co-creative relationships with the natural world.

I left Findhorn in 2004 and moved to Australia, and after several years break, again felt a call – this time towards a fledgling group wanting to start an ecovillage on the Central Coast of New South Wales, an hour and a bit north of Sydney.

Called Narara, it is now well on the way to incarnating in a beautiful valley with Permaculture as a major theme.

NOTE: *John Talbott, an English major and engineer, first came to Findhorn in 1978 for a year; he stayed for 25. Inspired by Findhorn's aspiration to co-create with nature, John became a champion of all things ecovillage, pioneering and developing the concept of sustainable communities first in Findhorn and later as a founder member of the Global Ecovillage Network. Author of "Simply Build Green", a technical manual of ecological building, John now resides in Sydney, Australia - working on his second ecovillage in Narara on the NSW central coast.*

PART TWO

Peoplecare

*Expect only the very best in everything and everyone, and see it
come forth. Keep your heart open to one another. Look for the
highest good in each other, and work from that higher level of
consciousness. Encourage one another in every way possible; every
soul needs encouragement.*

— *EILEEN CADDY*

Modern psychology and spiritual enquiry come together in supporting healthy human development, just as in a Permaculture garden, where nothing is wasted or disrespected; all elements are integrated, one cycle leads to another, and the compost heap is valued as much as the food produced.

Spiritual enquiry reveals many unresolved patterns within our lives, which need to be creatively composted otherwise they lead to dysfunctional attitudes that weaken healthy human interaction.

Processes such as Psychosynthesis, Process Orientated Psychology and Non Violent Communication assist us in integrating them creatively, leading to healthier communities where all voices are heard and respected just as in a garden all plants are seen to have beneficial functions.

Supporting and nurturing places of observation, both in nature and in purpose-built structures is primary to deepen one's connectivity. It began a long time ago, when we first harnessed the element of fire, sitting around campfires. Giving us a sense of safety and protection, it warmed our bodies, soothed our hearts, and settled our minds, opening to that place of primordial memory.

We began to tell stories to one another about how it all began. Myths and legends, heroes and villains arose from those burning embers. There were times of wild creative rhythms transporting us beyond our physical limitations. Then silence settled, we listened to the vastness of the heavens above us and the depth of the earth below.

From that nomadic place we began to settle, constructing shelters, nurturing plants, animals, and caring for one another.

Today as we continue on this journey, a simple candle lit with intention opens up pathways to the heart. Silence is respected, cultivating the voice of intuition.

There is still a place for the campfire's song calling us back to that first remembrance, awakening our cellular memory to the present moment.

Simple times of reflection or meditation are vital if we are to listen to our inner voice and that of our place in the cosmic story.

Peoplecare is about looking after us as people, not just the world we live in. It works on both an individual and a community level. Self-reliance, co-operation and support of each other should be encouraged. It is, however, important to look after our selves on an individual level too.

Our skills are of no use to anyone if we are too tired to do anything useful! Peoplecare is also about our legacy to future generations.

This section looks at group processes and at individual nurturing. In an intentional community context there is always a dynamic between the needs of the fellowship and the needs of the individual, and how this is resolved is often crucial to the well-being of both.

CHAPTER SEVEN

Group Processes

*You need to have a vision of why you want to start a
community and then sound that note and those
who resonate to that note will be drawn to you.*
— *PETER CADDY in Faces of Findhorn.*

Most Permaculture design goes on in groups. I know of very few designers who work totally on their own. Most peoples' introduction to Permaculture is through the Permaculture Design Course (PDC), a 72-hour standard programme that earns those who complete it an international certificate.

Even though today an increasing number are taking this course online, we have observed that the dynamic of doing this course as a small group of between 10 and 20 participants has tremendous value, and we are certain that this enhances the course as a learning experience.

One way to learn is to observe and analyze what is happening in one's group. All of us have spent a good part of our lives in groups of various sorts – family, class, club and work group, but rarely have we taken time to stop and observe what is going on in the group, and ask why the members are behaving the way they are.

One of our main goals in Permaculture is to become better observers, as well as better participants. It is difficult both to observe and participate at the same time, and the development of our skill as participant/observer can only be gained by concerted practice.

Content and Process

In any group we will find the two main elements of content and process. Content is what is being said, the matter under discussion. There are things that can be seen or heard; gestures, tone of voice, expressions and so on. Feelings, concerns and attitudes are hidden and cannot be really known without checking with the persons concerned.

The content and these other observable things can help deduce feelings. Our own "feeling" can sometimes help us to enquire about the unseen areas that affect the group life.

Process is what is happening to the group itself, the way things are being accomplished. Often these very important aspects of group work are ignored, and then the efficient working of the group is undermined. The content may be seen as the part of an iceberg out of the water, while the process is the part under the water, not easily seen but very important and influential.

It is necessary to recognize that in any group there are certain basic issues that affect the work and life of the group and individuals within the group. They cannot be ignored or wished away; rather, they need to be recognized, and as the group develops, conditions of trust and openness can help channel these emotional energies into creative and helpful group effort.

What are these issues or problems?

- Problems of identity and acceptance within the group. Who am I in this group? Where do I fit in? What kind of behaviour is acceptable here? Do I belong?
- Problems of goals and needs of the group. What do I want from the group? Are its goals consistent with mine? What have I to offer the group to help?
- Problems of power, control and influence. Who is in charge? Who will control what we do? How much influence will I have?
- Problems of intimacy. How close will we get to each other? How personal will things be? How much can we trust each other?

These problems exist and the effective life of the group depends upon their acceptance and the way in which the group deals with them. The part played by each member of the group is dependent upon his or her response to these problems within the group. The following are some of the kinds of behaviour that are produced in response to the issues in the group. It's useful to watch for them:

- Taking leadership. Is anyone assuming or representing authority?
- Dependency. Are people leaning on the leader or on anyone who represents the authority?
- Counter-dependency. Are there participants resisting anyone who represents authority?
- Pairing. Are there participants seeking one or more supporters or like-minded friends from a sub-group in which the members support and protect one another?

- Fighting and controlling. Is anyone asserting personal dominance, attempting to get one's own way, to satisfy one's own needs, regardless of others?
- Withdrawing. Are there people taking no part in the group to escape the sources of an uncomfortable feeling?

This is by no means a full list. The important thing is to increase our skill in observing what is happening, for this helps us to understand and thereby to be more effective in our membership of a group.

We might call this the invisible side of Permacultural group processes, but in fact many of the clues we are looking for *ARE* visible and observable. Honing your powers of observation is a useful skill and a good exercise. Here are some clues to help us observe:

- Who talks? For how long? How often?
- Who do people look at when they talk?
- At the group?
- At one person? (possible supporter? - the authority?)
- At the floor?
- How do people speak? What tone of voice?
- Who talks after whom? Any small asides between couples?
- Who interrupts? Do they interrupt the same person constantly?
- What gestures are used?
- How do people sit?
- Any yawns, twiddling of thumbs, gazing out of windows?

The kind of observations we make can give us clues to other important things that may be going on in the group and are having a strong effect upon the life and work of the group.

Observation of group process helps us to develop awareness of others and of our effect upon them. Sharing and analyzing our observations ensures that they can be checked by others and also contributes to the development of new responses in the group.

One way of effectively sharing observations is for any group member to ask the group to look back on what has been happening, then for members to share their observations and check with one another in areas where checking is needed.

The Group Being

As a group comes together, it's like creating a soup. Each person brings their past history, talents and issues, and, whether consciously or not, adds these as their ingredients to the soup. For the most part we have no idea what soup we are creating, it's a bit like throwing the ingredients into a pot of water while blindfolded.

So usually the soup you create is a surprise. And you may like it as you start to taste it, or you may not. You may think, "Oh my God, this isn't what I thought it was going to be, this isn't what I wanted." At this point you have some options: You can stay while bemoaning the fact that you don't like your soup and you will feel stuck with it. Or you can walk out on it. Or, you can realize that you can take the blindfold off, turn around and examine all the ingredients and play with them, making it the most rich, nourishing and delicious soup you could possibly imagine.

When a group comes together, in it you have each of the individuals as themselves, but you also have something else, something that is more than just the sum of the individuals, and we can call this the Group Being. The Group Being is a multi-dimensional shared field of consciousness: the physical, psychological and spiritual environments of the group.

It is a composite of each person's beliefs, feelings, background, understanding, fears, purpose, direction, expectations, high dreams and low dreams, spoken and unspoken dreams and aspirations.

The group soup

A Norwegian Permaculture Design group celebrating a successful course!

In any group, and to some degree in all of humanity, all the common fears, dreams, loves and issues will be there. The interesting, exciting and possibly intimidating thing will be to see which of these themes and issues are strongest. Which are most wanting expression and exploration in this group so the members will grow as individuals, as a group and ultimately as humanity.

Roles

All groups and organizations have many roles within them. Some of these are identified, such as the leader or notetaker, but many are not identified as explicitly. We have these roles in our groups because they are a part of society as a whole. Individuals may be identified with only one particular role in a group.

It is helpful if we can become more fluid and learn to change roles. After all, we take different roles in life depending on the situation, with our children, with our parents, with our partner and with our colleagues at work. We are larger and more versatile than any one role. Yet we often get stuck in a role in our organizations.

Often, the roles get confused with the people who temporarily occupy them. When we do this, we tend to personalize conflicts, rather than view them as tensions between roles. This creates unnecessary hurt and prevents the organization from learning by processing the roles. Unless the role is addressed, it will remain.

Even if an individual leaves, the role remains and is filled by someone else. Examples of roles might be: leader, tyrant, disturber, outsider, fool, victim, rescuer, child, parent, minority, terrorist, organiser, and there are many more.

Awareness of the qualities or roles that are being represented in the group is a fundamental step in understanding the group consciousness. Some roles can be noticed by their absence.

Sometimes it is easier to think in terms of qualities or themes in looking for what is present in a group, such as conflict, resistance, harmony, detachment, attachment, sexuality, anger or frustration. If roles or qualities are strongly present in the group field, they need to be represented or played out or spoken for in the group.

Otherwise they will be in there in an underground way causing blockages of energy until usually, they explode out. The more mature a group, the more these roles are fluid and will move and be expressed by different people at different times.

The more the roles get polarized and expressed by only one or two people the more stuck in conflict the group may become. It may be difficult to channel energies that are not openly acknowledged in the group.

If this is happening, there are ways to help keep the roles and energy moving in the group:

- Awareness – we need to recognize that roles exist and then to name the ones being expressed or suppressed.
- Owning our reactions – if we are reacting with an emotional charge to something that is happening in the group, or to one of the group members, this is always a sign that we have something to learn from the situation or the person. See if you can become conscious of the exact nature of your reaction. Do you feel angry, withdrawn or afraid? Notice if this is familiar to you. Usually our reactions are very strong when we have had difficult experiences of a similar nature in the past. Who or what does the past situation remind you of?
- Recognizing and owning the role or quality in ourselves – most often when we react to a situation or a person, we are finding it hard to recognize and own that quality in ourselves. If you feel furious at how stubborn someone is being, look inside yourself and ask, "Where is my stubbornness? How and where do I express it?" If you feel frustrated or impatient at somebody who always wants to speak last, try to identify with them. What would happen if you did the same? Look also for your strong positive responses and try to recognize those qualities in yourself.
- Recognizing when somebody else is acting out for us – ask yourself, "Is this person expressing something that I am holding back? Am I not yet strong enough to be able to do this for myself?" If you can recognize and name it when this is the case, you have made a good start towards doing it for yourself.

It is always useful to cultivate an awareness of microcosm and macrocosm. When reflecting on what is happening in a group and looking at the issues and roles being presented, it can be helpful to pause, stand back from the immediacy of the group, and look at what is happening in the world at that time.

Questions such as, "What is happening currently in our local community? What is happening on the world scene? What are the major issues and themes being played out?" See if you can find the commonality.

This will nearly always bring a deeper understanding of why certain issues are surfacing to be worked with within your group.

Visionary Leaders

Corinne McLaughlin, executive director of The Center for Visionary Leadership and a Fellow of The World Business Academy and the Findhorn Foundation in Scotland, has identified a series of qualities and characteristics of what she calls Visionary Leaders.

Visionaries often have wonderful dreams and can talk about them endlessly, but Visionary Leaders are able to actualize these visions. They take action to make them a reality, using effective strategies with achievable goals.

Visionary Leaders are pioneers who bring a new, compelling picture of the future into the present to create a meaningful purpose that meets people's needs. Visionary Leaders lead from the inside out. They:

- Courageously follow an inner sense of direction.
- Stand for core values and clear principles.
- Are aligned with their inner essence or higher purpose.
- Link people's current needs to their deeper, spiritual needs.
- Provide a larger context of meaning and purpose for others.
- Think creatively outside the norm and embrace challenges and change.
- Radiate energy and vitality.

Visionary Leadership is a quality of being. It is a synthesis of will, heart and mind. Visionary Leaders are effective in four dimensions:

- Spiritual - commitment to core values and service.
- Mental - creativity, intuition and vision.
- Emotional - empowering, supportive relationships.
- Physical - innovative, courageous action.

We have seen how the Findhorn Foundation Community was founded on the basis of spiritual guidance received by Eileen Caddy and Dorothy MacLean, which were then implemented by Peter Caddy. In the early years the community relied on this trio for all decisions.

However, one day Eileen was told not to give guidance any more so that the community could develop the maturity to stand on its own feet. Once again, the transition was difficult, but today the community is strong and self-reliant, and Eileen is still highly respected, even many years after her death.

The late Peter Caddy gave the following advice about how to go about founding a community:

> *"People often ask me how to go about starting a community such as Findhorn. One way you don't do it is by advertising for others to come and join you. That's putting the cart before the horse, and it's not the way to attract people anyway. The people are important and what they are is more important than what they know, but first you must have a vision."*
>
> — *Faces of Findhorn.*

Providing visionary leadership creates a focus for a group and history is full of examples. Indeed, it does seem that most groups need this in order to get started, but there are also many examples where the leadership can be too strong, and the power that such leadership gives to the leader may put them off course.

Communities develop and change over time and where strong visionary leadership can be invaluable in founding a new group, it may be very counter-productive later on.

Group Development

Groups and communities are social organisms, which behave according to patterns that we can see and recognize in all of life. Groups move from youthfulness, through maturity, and into old age. In considering the life cycles of human beings and human groups, there are instructive parallels in the natural world.

Matching patterns found in nature to those in systems that we design for ourselves helps us understand those systems better.

By using Permaculture and tracing patterns from the natural world onto things that we are designing, we might draw a parallel between the initial stages of communities and the vegetable garden. Mulch and compost are applied to the soil and micro-organisms begin to multiply. Compost heaps heat up to such a degree that

Dancing at the Scandinavian Permaculture gathering in 2011.

they have occasionally been known to burst into flames.

From this chaotic state biological action creates humus out of the raw biomass. The initial stages of a community might also be experienced as chaotic: ideas come and go, things happen fast, opportunities present themselves and need to be utilized. There are hectic days, long hours; it's stressful but exciting.

The pioneering era is often the most exciting period of a community's existence, and memories of it will linger on nostalgically. The wish to remain young is understandable, but, like people, communities grow and mature, and the behaviour that was fine when young becomes inappropriate in someone older.

One characteristic of new groups working together is that most of the members can tackle most of the jobs. Work is shared out fairly informally, and everyone lends a hand where it is needed. Shared work builds community, and the memory of it is often embellished to create the "golden age" legends that in later life sustain the community.

A community has its own biography, and what happens at the beginning of its life will affect subsequent growth and development. Each individual member will create direct personal links with many different areas, giving them a feeling that this is "my place". Stories emerge as part of the oral history that gets told and retold as the years go by.

A community is on a journey. An intentional community is a group moving through time, usually with aims having to do with social or personal renewal. Just as on a journey you will stop and refer to the map, check the compass, and make sure that the direction is still right, so might a community take time out to check if the course is being followed.

Unfortunately communities can't remain youthful for too long; either infant mortality sets in and the community disintegrates, or they mature.

In the development of the human being, something happens in the years between about the age of 14 and 21 that establishes the person's identity. This period is often regarded as difficult. Christianity recognizes the beginning of this period in the ceremony called Confirmation, literally confirming the young person's faith.

Judaism does likewise with the Bar Mitzvah, also reaffirming the commitment of the individual to his or her religion. We are not suggesting that a community needs to wait nearly a decade and a half before establishing its own identity and self-awareness, but there is a crossover point, when the young and lively group that pioneered the original impulse becomes more mature, more sure of itself and its direction.

We have seen that one of the characteristics of the pioneering phase is that most members can do most jobs. As the community grows and matures, the increasing complexity of running a major enterprise will require a greater degree of specialization.

This should be accepted as part of the maturing process that a group goes through. As the community matures, specialization and professionalization should be well-established features of the group.

The experience of birth and death within the community will help the community to mature. Community support for the sick and dying also has a strong bonding effect in most cases.

Many communities begin their lives as a group of younger people, with a relatively small spread of ages. If the community remains small, and is unable to recruit regularly as it ages, this will result in a generation bulge rising up through the decades.

This could lead to serious problems when most of the members are older, unless there are well worked-out pension schemes or other safeguards against the time when the members can no longer work full-time. Active and on-going recruitment is another characteristic of the mature community.

There is a price to growth and development. We may move on to become more mature, but we will have to leave behind the characteristics of youth. The price of not growing, however, is even higher. People, and communities, need to move on, to grow and develop. It's OK to grow up.

When dealing with the issues of specialized work, recruiting new members, or creating good spaces for both the young and the old, we sometimes hear comments from the founder members: *"We didn't do it like this in the beginning; why do we need to change now? Aren't we losing our ideals?"* An awareness of the processes of change can help a community through those potentially conflict-filled changes.

Old age in the context of community development may look like the dissipation of collective ideals, and some commentators conclude that there is inevitability in the demise of the cooperative dream. Are we who live in community doomed to end up either forgotten, or as a display case in a museum?

The truth is that most communities don't last very long; only a handful continue for more than a century. As far as we know, only the Hutterites can claim a history longer than 200 years, and they have been going for 400!

Living Ideas

Some years ago the International Communal Studies Association held a conference in Israel that Jan attended, and the post-conference tour visited the first kibbutz, Degania, founded in 1910.

There must have been at least 15 nations represented in the visiting group, a mixture of academics and activists. The air was thick with Ph.Ds and professors. And here they all were, hearing about the founders of the first kibbutz, about their ideals and how they took these ideals and translated them into everyday life.

This was for us a great example of how the idea lives on, how it is cared for by those who record and preserve the stories of the past, and who then hand those stories on to new listeners. Who knows what effects this short visit had? Which of these activists heard a story or an idea, and brought it back to their home community, where it was heard again by those who today are struggling with the challenge of creating community? Which of these academics heard a fact that later would emerge in some article or lecture on the inner workings of communal life?

How do we measure the success of a community? It is not merely longevity. We need to look at the social ecology of the group, its relationship to other groups, to other sectors of society, and to society as a whole. We might look at intentional communities as bearers of ideas, ideas that have as their intention the creation of positive change in the mainstream.

All plants live off decaying organic matter in the soil, turning it into nutrients for themselves. A similar process happens in community. As a community breaks up or decays, individuals leave for other things. Many go back into mainstream society, get jobs, maybe get married and buy a small family house.

Others move on to other projects, and other communities. Whatever they do, they take with them their experiences of communal living, and this will inevitably influence their later lives. The decay of the older project will become educational nourishment for new ones.

One of the images that helps us to contemplate the significance of intentional community is that of the river. In youth the river is lively, noisy, and vigorous as it rushes down the mountainside.

In maturity it is grand and stately, winding through rolling countryside, watering the meadows and supporting great trees along its banks. In old age the river creates deltas and finally empties itself into the sea, losing itself in the ocean.

Without rivers, though, the ocean would dry up through evaporation, which is what is happening with the Dead Sea, the Caspian, and the Aral Sea, where the rivers flowing into these seas have been diverted for irrigation. Rivers keep the ocean alive.

In a similar way, intentional community keeps society alive; it contributes social impulses and social renewal. They say that a great river such as the Amazon can be detected over 200 miles out to sea by the colour and freshness of the water. In a similar way, some communities may be detected many decades later by the social changes they create.

Bearing this in mind, we may see the gradual dissolution of old age to be a hopeful sign of social renewal rather than depressing symptoms of decrepitude.

This is for us the real meaning of sustainability: the ability of our ideals to live on, to inspire others, to give meaning and to recreate society. It is in the end sustainable eco-communities that will create sustainable ideals and the sustainability of our ideals that will create a sustainable society.

Community celebrations in Findhorn.

The Weave of Permaculture and Community

I GREW UP IN TWO CULTURES. My family moved from Norway to London in the mid-1950s, my father being the London correspondent for one of Norway's leading newspapers for nearly two decades.

We spoke Norwegian at home, and I spoke English at school and with my friends. In my teens I developed a strong interest in archaeology and geography, which I went on to study at university.

The late 1960s and early 1970s were strong times to live through. The atomic bomb hung over us, young Americans were going to Vietnam and getting killed. We were in an uproar. This wasn't the world we wanted. I got involved in alternative communities.

I met Ruth, my partner ever since. She was Jewish, I was a practicing Christian, and she added a third culture to my life.

We became teachers and moved into the country, finding a kind of community in self-sufficiency. We made our first attempts at growing our own food, having trouble that spring with differentiating between the cabbages and the weeds as things sprouted. We worked with others in appropriate technology and staged an exhibition in Nottingham city centre.

Our interest for intentional community led us to spending over a year on an Israeli kibbutz, adding depth to our Jewish culture, and bringing us into contact with Arabs in the Middle East. On our return to England we moved into deeper rural Lincolnshire. Ruth worked with a naturopathic doctor, I took an agricultural education, and we opened a whole-food cooperative shop (which is still going strong over 30 years later!).

We never found the intentional community we wanted in the United Kingdom. I was actively involved in several projects, but none of them really touched our hearts, so in the mid-1980s we moved back to the kibbutz.

In a way it was a kind of compromise. We wanted a large, well-run alternative community movement, which we found in the kibbutz. Over 250 cooperative villages strung out over the whole country, with their own research and education centres, their own banking system, and several generations of experience. We gave up on some of our ideals, organic wholefoods, do-it-yourself technology, "small is beautiful" thinking and spirituality.

The kibbutz movement was firmly based in the old paradigm, its traditions

Jan Martin Bang

set during the 1930s and '40s, and they were not easy to change. But it was alternative, anti-capitalist, democratic, participatory, and I felt welcomed. In addition, living as a practising Christian in a Jewish community with Muslim friends and neighbours gave me a direct experience of interfaith dialogue, a chance to meet people of different religions without having to be either defensive or missionizing.

For my first few years I worked in heavily industrialized agriculture, but gradually my old aspirations returned, and I moved into working with environmental education, for the children in our community and for students from abroad.

In the early 1990s I realized that the kibbutz movement, with its 270 villages and 150, 000 people, didn't have an environmental department. I requested, and got, an office at one of the movement's research institutes, gave it the name "The Green Room" and began to visit different kibbutz villages, giving talks and encouraging local environmental groups to set up projects; sorting garbage, recycling, composting, growing small vegetable plots with the children, and generally gathering information and raising awareness.

At about this time Permaculture arrived in Israel, two Australian brothers settled there and began to give talks and presentations, and arranged for Bill Mollison, and a little later, David Holmgren, to visit and tour. A little later I was offered the opportunity to learn Permaculture, organize two Permaculture Design Courses in Israel and given a laptop to be able to connect with the larger Permaculture and Ecovillage international networks.

During my first PDC, at The Farm in Tennessee, I had a series of "Aha" experiences, as all the varied ingredients of my life fell into an ordered pattern and gave me a whole range of tools for designing and thinking.

The breadth and depth of archaeology gave me time references stretching tens of thousands of years back. A large part of my geography studies had involved geomorphology; the study of landscapes, of reading the countryside as a book. From self-sufficiency I brought practical skills in building, growing food and managing resources. My studies of intentional community, both in Britain and in Israel, gave me a framework for how communities develop.

My meetings with people of different faiths, and those with none, inspired me to become involved in creating alternative lifestyles which included a space for spirituality, not specifically religious, but more free flowing, tolerant and open.

⁕

This was all confirmed when I attended the first two PDC courses that Graham Bell taught in Israel. I saw this foundation course as a serious agent for social change, with its emphasis on practical tasks and taking responsibility: how this is best done in community in its widest sense, and how Permaculture could develop the way we think.

Our lives led us to leave the kibbutz after 16 years, and we moved on to a Camphill village in Norway, where we finally found the missing spiritual ingredient, within a network of over 120 anthroposophical village communities in more than 20 countries around the world. The insights of Rudolf Steiner enriched my Permaculture and added another dimension to it.

I taught some of the first PDC courses in Hebrew in Israel. In addition I have led seminars for Arabs in Israel, and Palestinians in Palestine, and in Cyprus and Turkey. Over the last decade I have facilitated the PDC in pioneering situations in Latvia, Iceland and remote parts of Norway.

Every time I see how important community is for social change. The skills and design tools we share with participants are always enhanced when used in group situations.

Permaculture brings in the elements we need for change, the invisible community glue makes them real.

CHAPTER EIGHT

Spiritual Nurturing and Enquiry

*Primarily, Findhorn is a spiritual centre, based on guidance
from higher levels and on esoteric teachings. It has a deliberate
focus on transformation and on exploring the frontier of a
new consciousness as part of a greater planetary unfoldment.*
— *Faces of Findhorn, 1980* .

In the old Materialist Reductionist paradigm, there arose a tradition that hard science and religion were implacably opposed to each other. In recent years this has resulted in provocative statements from such people as Richard Dawkins, who maintains that since we discovered science, "God is dead".

The real cutting edge of research by physicists indicates that all matter is at the same time energy, and that this energy seems to be interlinked in such a way that information is instantaneously shared throughout creation at a subatomic level.

What is interesting is that this is reflected in statements made by mystics from many established, mainstream religions. In science, matter and energy have become interchangeable. In the new paradigm, matter and spirit have become two sides of the same coin.

Interspirituality

When we dig down into the major established world religions, and get to their mystical aspects, there are many similarities. Combine this with a growing openness to dialogue between religions, and we arrive at a completely new phenomenon, the idea of "Interspirituality".

To be sure, there are today serious conflicts between some religions. As we write, the Islamic State in the Middle East dominates the news with atrocities carried out in the name of sectarian religion. In Northern Ireland we have had a conflict between Catholics and Protestants over many generations.

When we look closely at these conflicts, we might discern that politics, power and competition for space and resources are using the religious divisions to fuel

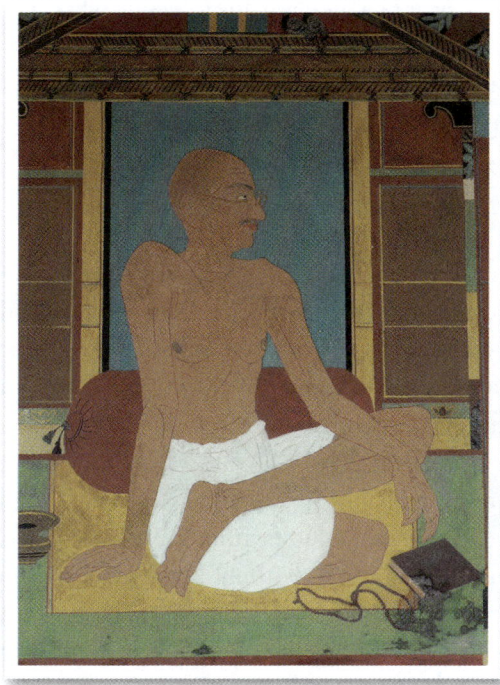

Portrait of Gandhi

the violence. Despite these conflicts, there have been serious attempts at dialogue between religions, and the number of interfaith organizations has leapt from three in 1945 to over 2, 000 by 2010.

In the book *The Song of the Earth,* where the above statistic is taken from, Will Keepin describes the work of the Snowmass Conference, a group of religious leaders from the main world religions, who have been meeting regularly for decades.

They have explored not just their similarities, but also found that their differences are leading them to new insights into their respective faiths and at the same time bringing them closer together in understanding each other.

This has tremendous implications when it comes to understanding the words "religious" and "spiritual". The word "religious" certainly implies relating to a specific tradition; Judaism, Roman Catholicism, Zen Buddhism or any other defined religion.

In the Concise Oxford Dictionary "religion" is defined as:

"One of the prevalent systems of faith and worship."

This means a definite set of rules, rituals and modes of thinking, praying and/or meditating. For many people, religion helps to define who they are as individuals, and relates them to a defined and recognizable group.

Spiritual, on the other hand, is much more general, a way of thinking, a view of the world, a paradigm. The Concise Oxford Dictionary defines "spiritual" as:

"Of spirit as opposed to matter, inner nature of man."

So we can be spiritual without necessarily following a specific religion. There is no doubt that spirituality is growing, at least in the western world, a world that has been dominated by a hard science that has denied the existence of spirit. This is exactly where we can see the new paradigm growing and taking shape. Some people maintain that the established religions have missed the boat, and are a hindrance to the new emerging spirituality.

Thomas Berry argues this in the same book, *The Song of the Earth*. Not everyone will agree with that, and we might look within the established religions for signs of spiritual renewal and more holistic environmental awareness.

In a recent issue of Resurgence and Ecologist magazine, November/December 2014, Adam Weymouth reports how the World Council of Churches, representing 590 million people, voted to remove their investments in companies without ethical commitments to tackle climate change.

This may not in itself mean that all those churches have turned into New Age congregations practicing Permaculture in their churchyards, but it does mean that we should regard them as partners in building a new sustainable future.

Bede Griffiths, in his book *Universal Wisdom*, clearly appreciates this new relationship between established religions:

"The religions of the world are meeting today in a way they have never done before… not in terms of rivalry and conflict but in terms of dialogue and mutual respect."

In every one of these religions the divine reality is present, and represented by particular symbols, and cultivated or worshipped by particular gestures, dances, movements, objects and texts. Buildings are elaborately constructed and decorated to reinforce these particular traditions.

Peeling all these trappings away will reveal a common core, a realization and understanding that at root, every religion is about the relationship of humanity, both as a whole and as each individual, to the whole of creation and its underlying forces and powers.

Religions can no longer remain isolated. Each one is a unique revelation of the eternal truth, manifested under specific historical, geographical and ecological conditions. Meeting in mutual respect with an openness to understand, and not to missionarize, religions have much to learn from each other's similarities and differences.

M. K. Gandhi was an early believer in interfaith dialogue. He says the following about all faiths being equal:

> *"I believe in the fundamental truth of all the great religions of the world. I believe they are all god-given and I believe that they were necessary for the people to whom these religions were revealed and I believe that, if only we could all read the scriptures of the different faiths from the standpoint of followers of these faiths, we should find that they were at bottom all One and were all helpful to one another."*
>
> *(This quote was found at Birla House, the M. K. Gandhi memorial in New Delhi.)*

Diversity of Belief Systems within Findhorn

Within the Findhorn Foundation community there is a great diversity of belief and practice. Some of these are really cultural, like Scottish country dancing and some of the celebrations of seasons and cycles.

Others are more esoteric like the Arcane school, the marriage of psyche and soul, and the Sacred Five Rhythms dance. Being Still and Co-creation with nature can be done nearly anytime and in any place, while the "Work that Reconnects" and David Spangler's wholism might be regarded as more analytical and rational.

The Findhorn Foundation grew out of the Western mystery school tradition tracing its roots back to the Egyptian mysteries through to the Essenes and Greece, the Albigensians, the Knights Templar, the Rosicrucians, the Theosophical Society and the Arcane School.

It created a fertile breeding ground for the next wave of spiritual enquiry that emerged in the 1960s through many people exploring pathways and practices in Asia and the Himalayas.

There were also those who were exploring indigenous cultures with their shamanic traditions and rituals, which spoke of everything being sacred, all life being connected by invisible threads and relationships. Sacred songs and dances from around the world came together in celebration of the beauty and the mystery of life. The seasons and cycles of nature anchored us to the lands of Northeast Scotland.

Gathering at the Findhorn Earth Lodge.

Then there was another great wave that arose to complement and ground all of the spiritual activity. This was modern psychology, which gave us the tools to integrate our unresolved biographical material that arose through meditation practices. Psyche and soul were seen as partners, deepening our communication with one another and the natural worlds.

Main sanctuary in Findhorn.

Findhorn today is both sacred and profane. You can sit softly in a multitude of sacred spaces both indoor and out, or use whatever techniques for centring yourself that fits both your psyche and soul. Taking a walk through the coastal sand dunes out to the cold vastness of the North Sea is just as nurturing as sitting in silent reflection.

If you are a body person there is yoga of many schools, or sacred dance gently guiding you into a place of peace and harmony. If you need to sweat your prayers then there is wild and ecstatic dance.

All work departments start with a silent attunement, focussing on the present moment. Then listening to the fellow co-workers and how they are feeling before starting the tasks at hand, with an attitude of mindfulness and service. We also tune out giving thanks for all that has taken place and the opportunity to serve with a simple attitude of *work is love in action*.

Spirituality is infused into *PEOPLE CARE*, caring for the whole person; your physical body, your emotional body, your mental body and your soul body. They are all to be expressed, integrated and respected.

Community and the Individual

When designing for community living, one of the most important features is the polarity between the needs of the community and the needs of the individual. This kind of duality manifests in many different ways and we might see this as a series of dualities:

- Individual and collective
- Community and consciousness
- Inner and outer

Globally we are transitioning from an age of separation to an age of reconnection. We see this clearly in the new paradigm, pioneered by the new physics that showed us how everything is connected to everything else. This is now underpinning a great deal of cutting edge thought.

In many intentional communities we now find an awareness of self-transformation in a collective context. Karen Litfin calls sustainability "an inside job", meaning that this is an inner work of personal transformation. Her thinking joins many others who realize that in order to create or design a sustainable culture, we need first to change the way we see, experience and know the world, a job which has to be done from within.

Rudolf Steiner addresses this dualism in a verse that is often quoted within the Camphill villages:

Health and wholesomeness only come
when in the mirror of the soul of man
the whole community takes shape;
And in the community lives
the strength of every single soul.

Taking Personal Responsibility

Jon Kabat-Zinn, researcher and teacher of mind/body interaction, tells an interesting anecdotal story about Buckminster Fuller, designer and inventor of the geodesic dome, in his book *Wherever You Go There You Are.*

Apparently Fuller did not have an easy early life, and he became quite depressed by how things were turning out for himself in his early thirties. He got as far as contemplating suicide, but after thinking about this for a while he decided that instead he would regard himself as dead, not worry about anything personally and devote himself to doing what was right for the planet.

He would continuously ask himself the question:

"What is it on this planet that needs doing that I know something about,
that probably won't happen unless I take responsibility for it?"

This fulfils one of the central tenets of the Permaculture ethic of taking personal responsibility, while still keeping a global and planetary consciousness. It also cuts across the frustration that often occurs when people build up attachment to specific outcomes of community decisions.

Our experience here is that when we detach ourselves from the often polarized sides of a discussion, and instead focus on helping the group to come to an agreement acceptable to everyone, this is helpful both to us, and to the outcome.

Deep Ecology

The Norwegian philosopher Arne Næss created the concept of Deep Ecology, which was subsequently further developed by a number of other writers. Næss found that there were many what he called Shallow Ecologists who were highly active in the environmental movement.

Deep Ecology

Shallow Ecologists were concerned about the world, active in conservation and protection, but they regarded the world as somehow being for the benefit of mankind, that humans stand central. For instance, we protect the rain forests to maintain the atmospheric balance so that *we* can breathe easily. We try to limit fossil fuel emissions because climate change is troublesome and expensive for us.

Næss wanted to go beyond this anthrocentric approach and so developed what he called Deep Ecology. Næss thought that Deep Ecologists are relatively few and far between, and they regard human beings as merely one of an enormous number of created beings, all of which are woven together in the vast tapestry of life.

All things are of intrinsic value *of themselves*, and protection is extended to all beings for the value of the whole.

This core concept of Deep Ecology created quite a stir, especially for those Christians who see themselves as God's appointed stewards of creation, and for some Anthroposophists, who see the development of human self-awareness as the highest pinnacle of freedom yet achieved in the physical world.

A little bit of controversy is of course healthy and good, and we all welcome a good discussion. For us as Permaculture designers, it is the developmental process of Deep Ecology that has value. Whether Deep Ecology is "true" or not, and what kind of value we attach to "deep" or "shallow" is not really of interest to us.

We find it most useful to present Deep Ecology as a way of looking at the world, a picture or an image of what might be going on. If by looking at this image and sharing it with others we arrive at a greater understanding, it has served its purpose.

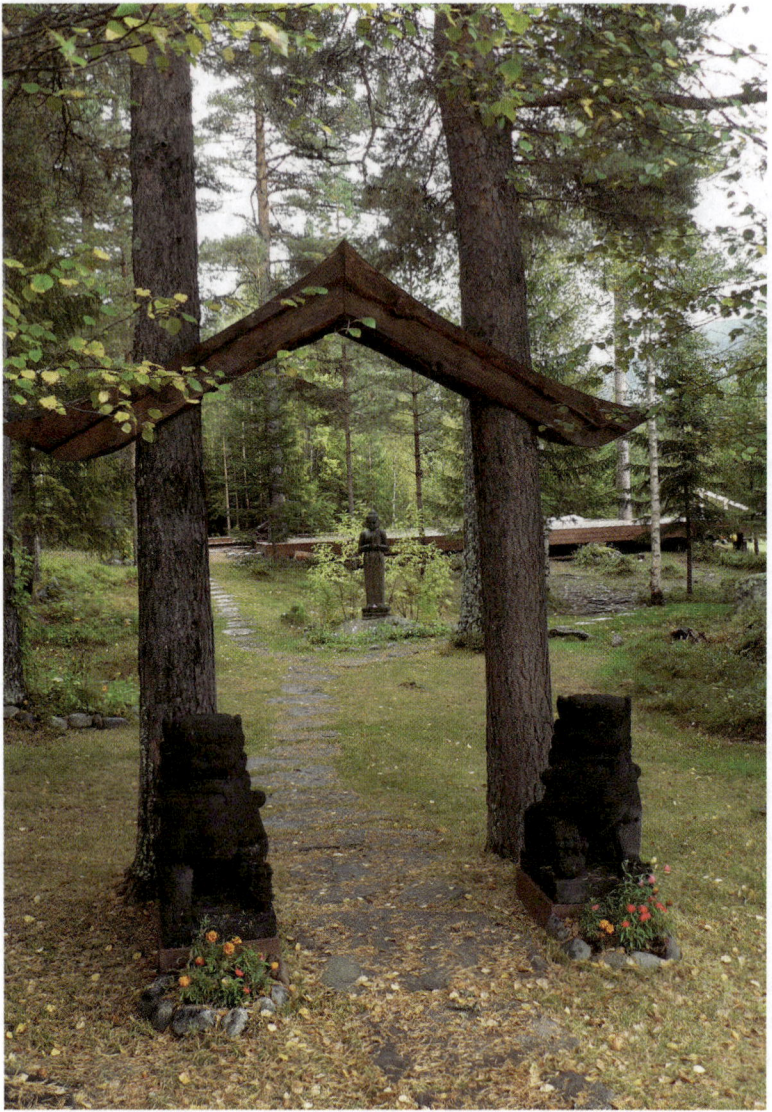

At the Meditation Centre "Dharma Mountain" in Norway.

If it stirs up conflicts and misunderstandings, it's better to put it aside and move on to other things.

Arne Næss was a skilled climber, as well as being the youngest appointed Professor of Philosophy in Norway. As a climber he was well aware of the effect of being exposed to stupendous nature, and his starting point for developing Deep Ecology was the Deep Experience.

This he describes as a spontaneous phenomenon, a realization of the wholeness of nature as a Gestalt, and an experience of the smallness of the human individual within the vast web of nature.

In the Deep Ecology process this Deep Experience leads to Deep Questioning, where ultimate norms are looked at, where one's own lifestyle is reconsidered, and where concrete decisions are taken. This questioning has led to the development of the Deep Ecology Platform, and to Deep Commitment.

The Deep Ecology Platform has subsequently been worked and reworked, and ardent followers of this path have now gone "beyond the platform", forging exciting new paths in the philosophical world. The Deep Commitment can be seen as one of the philosophical foundations of Permaculture, where change in behaviour is the result of thinking about the world and understanding how it works.

This is a serious philosophical foundation for Permaculture for those who find that important. In practical terms it slows down those impatient technical people who rush in and want to "get on with it!"

We might see the Deep Ecology process as follows:

- Deep experience
- Deep questioning
- Deep commitment
- Deep ecology platform
- Beyond the platform

Deep Ecology is thus a useful addition to the Permaculture tool chest, a process that can help individuals assess whether they want to stay at a level where we humans regard ourselves as the most important element in nature, or whether we want to go deeper into the new paradigm, where everything is connected to everything else on a level playing field.

Permaculture and Spirituality

The implications of introducing spirituality into the Permaculture concept opens up whole new dimensions. As we saw earlier, it's really important to be aware of the difference between spirituality and religion.

Devout Christians or Buddhists may want to define a Christian or Buddhist Permaculture, and we would welcome people who want to specialize within Permaculture. We already have this in other aspects; Urban Permaculture, Social Permaculture and other themes such as ecological economics or environmental building.

The spiritual path at the Meditation Centre "Dharma Mountain" in Norway.

Inevitably, a subject as large and diverse as Permaculture will split up into specific areas, where specialists in their fields will go deeper into their subjects.

An openness to spirituality, in tune with and as part of the new paradigm, would be very welcome within Permaculture, giving it a new dimension, a new perspective, and anchoring the technical design aspects of Permaculture firmly within the new way of looking at the world which we need in order to solve the problems that the old paradigm have created.

This would also anchor Permaculture firmly into what is happening in the western world today, where great numbers of people are searching for a new meaning in their lives, a meaning that is deeper and more profound than the shallow consumerism offered by the prevailing social ethos.

Also in other areas of the world, in societies based much more on traditional foundations, with religious rituals and beliefs being practised at a local community level, the recognition of a spiritual component would help to make Permaculture more acceptable and recognizable.

❦

Most people on this planet have some kind of spiritual component in their lives. When they recognize that Permaculture offers a meeting place where this can be the subject of a positive and respectful dialogue, we will have created an edge where new ideas can be developed, and new alliances forged.

PERSONAL STORY · HELENE C. BØHLER

Resting in Natural Being —
Tai Chi and Permaculture

WHEN I FIRST MET with Rising Dragon Tai Chi many years ago, I found a path which invited me in to a deeper connection with myself, and with my being in the world.

A place where I felt at home. It is an evolving and deepening journey. Along the way I have also discovered Permaculture, and feel it resonates in many ways with Tai Chi. In both paths I have felt that new realizations and deeper understanding is something which somehow is already known, even if it is the first time I hear it, like it's my body/nature that knows.

I feel this recognition of something already known in itself illustrates the universal truths from the foundations of both Tai Chi and Permaculture; the inherent wisdom and truth in nature.

The essence of Tai Chi is not something constructed, it is already there innate in us and in the world. We are already nature, so we are not separate. All we need to do is remember, and listen, *"We are already that which we seek."*

When I listen into where I am in this moment, I can feel more clearly where natural being wants to move me. The action emerges from this moment, not as a fixed rule, but as action rooted in nature. In a similar way permaculture design

Helene Bøhler

arrives out of the specific situation, and listening to what is already there, rooted in natural dynamics and cycles.

When we become aware of our presence, it is easier to act naturally in the world, rather than being in re-action. Action without listening often creates more complex situations, whether this is on the small scale, personally, or on the big scale, like in some of the symptoms we are experiencing with the current state of the planet.

The natural action that arises from listening means I am not standing in the way, and so also helps to conserve energy, the path of least resistance, both in Tai Chi and in Permaculture terms, as human be-ings; to be part of the solution and not the problem.

NOTE: *Helene Bøhler organized the Nordic Permaculture Festival in 2013, where the Norwegian Association celebrated 25 years since its foundation. She is now chair of the board of the Association, and is organizing a nationwide directory of Permaculture study, research and visitor sites. She is pursuing a diploma in Permaculture based on this.*

PART THREE

Fairshare

*There should be no discrimination in love, for divine love
embraces all alike. It sees all people in my image and likeness, no
matter what colour, race, sex, creed or religion. You will have to
reach the point when you can see and understand the oneness of
all life, know the true meaning of the family of all human beings,
and know Me as the source of all.*

— EILEEN CADDY

The Permaculture ethic of Fair Share brings the Earth Care and People Care ethics together. We only have one Earth, and we have to share it – with each other, with other living things, and with future generations.

This means limiting our consumption, especially of natural resources, and working for everyone to have access to the fundamental needs of life – clean water, clean air, food, shelter, meaningful employment and social contact.

Limiting our consumption sounds like it might not be much fun; limiting anything is not so much fun. Clearly this is going to be a hard sell. If instead we start from the position of abundance and sharing, we could package this to sound like fun, and that's what we need to do.

We have been told continuously that there are too many of us humans, that there's too little food and resources to go round, and that we have to limit ourselves. This maintains a feeling of scarcity, and is actually very good propaganda for the right wing monetarist ego and greed driven theorists who have dominated the world scene for the last thirty years.

We know from psychology that when people are confronted by bad news about the future, by the fear of an impending crisis, by the possibility that there will be shortages of food, water and space, that they go into an ego driven modus.

Most people will look out for themselves and their immediate family first. This is probably a very sound reaction, based on millennia of conditioning. This also helps the monetarist right wing economists and politicians expand and maintain their popularity, because people who feel threatened, go into ego modus, and support policies that divide people, while at the same time avoiding politics that encourage sharing.

We know from nature that we have abundance. Natural systems produce abundance by their very nature. In fact it seems to be one of the basic ecological laws that ecologies expand, creating more diversity and more abundance.

When offered abundance we go into sharing modus, which is also backed up by psychological research. When there is plenty to go round we tend to give freely to others, secure in our knowledge that we ourselves and our nearest family will not go short. This in turn promotes the economics of sharing and the politics of cooperation rather than competition.

So let's focus on abundance, upon the generosity of nature and Mother Earth, and look for joyful ways of enjoying this bounty together with as many people, animals, plants and ecosystems that we can.

CHAPTER NINE

Alternative Economics

Why not start right now thinking abundance? Realize that
there is no virtue in being poor. I want you to understand
that money as such is neither good nor bad; it just is.
It is there to be used, and it has to be kept circulating and
not hoarded. It is power, and power has to be used wisely.
— *EILEEN CADDY*

Thoughts About Money

Money is a token of an invisible reality. The money we use every day, coins, or bits of paper, and even more so, the cards and computers that now transfer something electronically, have no value in themselves, and cannot be used for very much except this monetary exchange exercise.

Money is, in essence, trust. We trust that the other partner in our exchange shares our belief in the value of the exchange. The Greeks called money "Numisma", which translated into English means consensus. We agree that the money tokens we use have certain values. This agreement is invisible. Who can "see" an agreement of this type?

The money is a token. When economists talk about the "reality" of economics, they actually are talking about a dream world, a dream world that not everyone agrees upon today.

There is actually no agreement and no consensus; the Occupy Wall Street demonstrations proved that decisively. Many people have lost faith in the main global and national banks and related financial institutions. Their traders are regarded as crooks that are cheating the system.

Recently a whole group of Wall Street traders were fined millions of dollars for insider trading on the currency markets. In other words, many of these traders working with and for the banks are convicted criminals.

This is the very stuff that threatens the institutions that make up the global economic system, which may be one reason why the state and the establishment do not want to admit that the economic system needs changing. After all, which emperor would want to admit that his "new clothes" are nothing at all?

Our use of these small symbolic tokens prove that behind the material world that we can sense with our fingers and put into our pockets and wallets, there exists an invisible world that is dependent upon our ideas and the agreements we make between us.

It is the invisible world of our consensus that is the foundation of the existence of coins and banknotes. Without this consensus, the economic system will be prone to periodic crashes, as often as our trust in the system no longer gives money its value. Indeed, the crisis of modern economics is that the invisible world is no longer reflected in the material world.

This is another reflection of the basis of the spiritual science of anthroposophy, which at its base posits a spiritual dimension that is the foundation of the physical material world. It is also a reminder that ecology, the natural system that underpins all life on this planet, has to be the foundation of all our practices.

Currently, many traditional economists think that it's the other way round, and consider the natural environment to be subject to economic "laws" that they make up. In this way of thinking, no value is given to natural environments except the value that can be exploited from them by our "economic" activities.

❧

The urgent need is to make the shift from the current situation, where ecology is a sub-set of economy, to one in which economy is a sub-set of ecology. Under this new scenario, the "environment" will no longer be a bank of inanimate resources for use in our various economic processes, but rather the living eco-system of which we form part and within whose limits we must learn, once more, to survive and thrive.

Again, we see that there is no need for a technical fix here. What is needed is a new way of thinking, a new paradigm, a new relationship to the natural world.

M. K. Gandhi says the following about economics:

> *"I must confess that I do not draw a sharp or any distinction between economics and ethics. Economics that hurt the moral well-being of an individual or a nation are immoral and therefore sinful. Thus the economics that permit one country to prey upon another are immoral."*

This quote was found at Birla House, the M. K. Gandhi memorial in New Delhi.

The Three Levels of Money

One way of creating a new way of thinking about money is to divide it into three levels of use. The first level is the day-to-day satisfaction of needs. Food, shelter and clothing all need to be purchased or traded. This is *consumption money*.

If we are a little careful, we may be able to save some of our money, after satisfying our basic needs, and this can be used to invest in projects that we dream up, plan and design. Often, such projects need material components provided either directly by nature, or by other people's work. This has to be paid for, and we can use our money for this. This is *investment money*, and we can say that this money "makes our dreams come true".

If we can save a little money from this, we may feel free to give it away to a charity, to a project or a worthy cause as a *free gift*. The giving of free gifts is as important for the giver as for the recipient. Gift economies have been practised by many cultures in the past, and have been studied by economists, showing that these are true economic systems.

They are a way of making sure that wealth moves around the community, that individuals have ways of both getting what they need, and giving from what they have produced. In short, it's just another way of trading goods and services.

It might be worth sitting down and planning your personal economy in this fashion, working out how much you need for *consumption*, how much is left for *investment*, and if you can set aside some for *free gifts*.

In the diversity we are seeking within the world of economics, based on our study of robust ecologies as having a high diversity, it's important to understand that also within the economic system, diversity is important to keep the system resilient. In our economic thinking, we must try to avoid a monoculture.

Business Motives

When thinking about new initiatives it is worth pondering the following angle: Is this new venture inspired by the realm of the spirit or does it come from a motivation from the realm of money?

If the primary aim is to make a profit, many things will be done that are based only on that priority. Clearly, any venture that has an economic or financial aspect needs to be able to pay the bills. As we often say in Permaculture, if we can't pay the bills, it's not Permaculture.

The distinction is in the primary aim. Are we making money by providing a service, or are we providing a service that needs to have its costs covered?

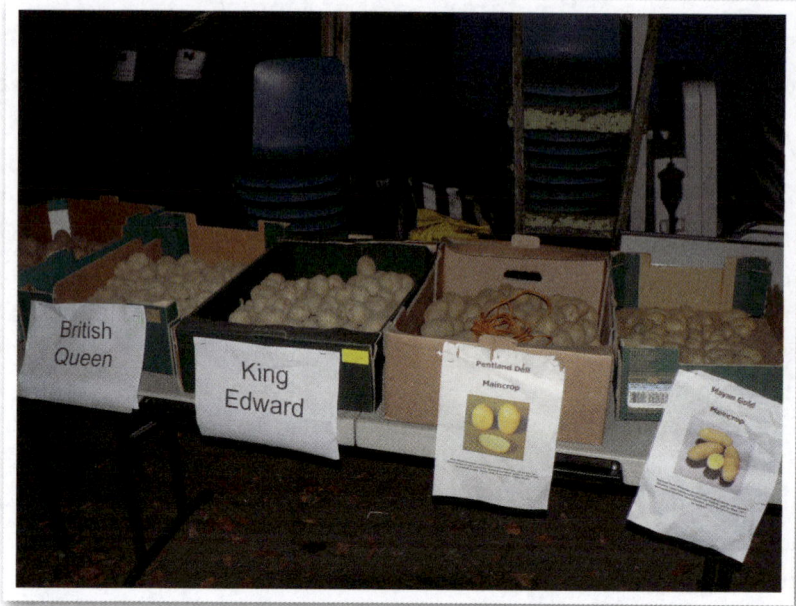

Trading seed potatoes at Transition Town Forres, inspired by the Findhorn
Community. The motive here is to provide a service to the community,
not to make a profit for the business.

It's not certain that all things that are money-inspired are bad or evil, but it's a good
thing to be clear about why we do things, and it makes a difference how we can get
other people involved.

A spiritually inspired venture will often get other participants and partners who
are motivated by how they can contribute, whereas a profit-inspired venture will get
people involved to the extent that they can profit from it themselves.

Spiritual Capital

Capital can be defined as wealth in the form of money or other assets. The last
words "other assets" open up a whole new spectrum of ideas as to what form capital
may take. Ethan Roland, writing in *Permaculture Magazine* in 2011, defines eight
forms of capital, including spiritual capital.

He goes further to suggest that the currency of spiritual capital is faith and
prayer, and that the aim is to achieve enlightenment.

Some of the other forms of capital he analyses are "intellectual", "experiential"
and "cultural". These ideas are meant to stimulate discussion and exploration rather
than being a "truth" about economics.

When considering human activities such as economics, it is important to be able to view them through different lenses, to see them in various ways, rather than regarding them as static and set in stone. The way we distribute goods and services are many and varied.

Biblical and Islamic Economics

In the Old Testament of the Bible, in the Book of Leviticus, strict rules are laid down to ensure that land and wealth is redistributed regularly.

The seven year cycle called Shmitta calls for the land to be rested, a kind of holy year for nature, echoing the call for the holy day of the Sabbath for human rest. The fifty year cycle of Joval, the origin of our modern word "Jubilee", calls for a redistribution of wealth, the redeeming of slaves and indentured labour, and the giving back of land that had been sold when families fell on hard times.

The basic idea was to create a balance between the efficiency of competition, and its negative aspects when wealth in money or land tended to become concentrated amongst only a few individuals.

In the Koran, trading and wealth are mentioned as highly positive things. They are also a test of one's faith. Clearly if a person is in great need or in distress, it might make sense to turn to God for help. Would we still remember God when we are wealthy and rich? Would the earthly pleasures that wealth could buy distract us from keeping God in our minds? In this way Islam uses wealth as a test of faith, wealth has a spiritual component, it's a tool on our spiritual path.

Non-Monetary Abundance or Fair Shares

The Findhorn Foundation was started by a small group of people dedicating their lives in service to humanity in co-creation with nature through following their inner guidance.

There was no monetary reward, just faith that all needs would be met. Everyone volunteered their time and energy, sharing meals and resources with a willingness to do what needed to be done.

There was a great sense of a non-monetary abundance, the more you gave the more you received.

The first communal building erected was the place to meditate in, and listen to music or inspirational people. It was open 24 hours a day for anyone to use. The next building was the community kitchen and dining hall where we shared all the cooking, serving and cleaning together.

There was food free of charge for anyone who wished to volunteer their time in

Community centre Findhorn.

service to the community. Everything was shared and whenever we needed more bed space we added another caravan.

In the mid-1970s we started building a large communal space for meetings, conferences, theatre, dance, ritual, celebration and meditation. All events were free to members of the community. There was such a sense of abundance and this still permeates the community today. You can choose to be a residential member of the educational trust or non-residential. Your basic living needs will be met and you will have the choice of how you will participate and support the overall community process.

Today there are dozens of co-operatives and social enterprises to choose from, besides all the study groups, dance groups, singing groups and hill-walking groups. They all have an underlying ethic of *"if it's not fun it's not sustainable"*.

Manifestation and Potential

One of the tools that is used in Findhorn is the "Law of Manifestation". This works out from each person's individual core being. I am what I think I am, I create myself through my thoughts about myself.

This is not a dreamlike wishful thinking fantasy, but a result of observation and clear thinking. As we create ourselves, we create our world around us. While being aware of this process it's extremely important to withstand the forces of advertising.

These are forces that try to create a different world, a world where the producer who pays for the advertising will profit economically, usually at our expense. Modern advertising tries to create a world where we are conditioned to want more and more of things that we really don't need, things that the producer is selling and making a profit by each sale. A great deal of advertising is aimed at creating a need for things that we really don't need.

When we try to create our own individual reality by our own means, we create an alternative to that consumer-driven world, an alternative that can be very different. The more we work with this, and connect with other individuals that are also working with the same or similar aims we create a community of ideals. We call this manifestation, because it will unfold around us, manifesting itself in our physical world.

In some ways it is just releasing potential that is already there. When we chop firewood, dry it and store it, it has the potential to heat us. All we need to do is to apply fire, and the potential heat will be released.

If we consider that divinity or enlightenment is within reach of the human being, then this is another potential we carry with us. We may not release it, but we have the possibility if we work with it in the right way. Manifestation is a process of releasing the potential that already exists.

Nature gives us abundance in many ways, being wealthy is seeing that abundance, even within poverty. In Permaculture we often talk about seeing the solution within the problem and releasing it.

In many ways, Nathan Roland was hinting at this in developing his ideas of spiritual capital; he was looking for the invisible, spiritual qualities within wealth that might make us all a little richer.

The Opportunity Within the Problem

When we looked at the challenges facing us in the world of technology, we saw that a transition to a green, renewable energy future has the potential to create many new jobs and business opportunities.

Here again, we can see that by turning a problem into a solution, and by seeing the potential within it, we can create an exciting new future that would be attractive also to the entrepreneur.

Communities can be busy, creating new jobs, replacing exploiting technologies with techniques that enhance and enrich the Earth. This is exactly what the natural ecologies do, as they grow, develop and expand. New niches are created all the time, which in turn are filled by new organisms that in turn create products that are nourishment for yet more organisms.

If we can create a new economic system that mimics this pattern, based on technologies that nurture the Earth and its inhabitants, both human and non-human, we will indeed create a bright new future for us all.

Ekopia

Our choice, as co-workers in the Findhorn Foundation, is to receive the same level of payment as our agreement towards equity. Another important way of sharing is Ekopia, our internal bank system of alternative currency.

Ekopia is a co-operative with over 250 members that provides a number of important community services. One of them is to provide an outlet for investment money.

The co-operative offers shares to members and friends of the community that are re-invested in various projects. These include the Phoenix Wholefoods Shop, an eco-chalet project, the community-owned wind turbines, various affordable housing projects and several local educational charities including the Moray Steiner School.

These shares attract a modest amount of interest. Overall about £1 million has now been invested in this way. Ekopia, which subscribes to the local code of business ethics, is in some ways similar to a microbank, although:

- It is under the control of its members who have one vote each regardless of their investment.
- Its activities must support a community interest rather than simply be 'for profit' in a general sense.

The local Findhorn currency: the Eko.

Ekopia also operates an alternative currency system called the Eko. This was launched in 2002 and today there are about 20,000 Ekos in circulation. Most of the main organizations in the community have agreed to accept Eko notes in exchange for goods and services rendered and people are encouraged to take a proportion of their wages in the currency.

Ekos are valued at par with sterling ie., 1 Eko = £1, and notes are issued in denominations of 1, 5, 10 and 20. The main aims & purposes of the Eko currency issue are:

- To provide low cost financing for new projects. Currently most of the cash so raised is invested in affordable housing.
- To promote local businesses, projects and the ecovillage in general as a place of innovation and sustainable economic activity.
- To inspire both guests and residents with the demonstration value of a locally based currency, and to get the users thinking about how and where they spend their money.
- To create gift capital for local businesses and projects. Issues are time-limited and the last one created a surplus of about £1,000 that was donated to various local projects.

Ekopia also seeks grants and has supported various projects by this means including researching affordable housing models and a youth exchange initiative to rural Bolivia. In 2014 an EU grant was received to enable the construction of a new office building to support business development in the community.

Ekopia participates in various national initiatives that promote community-based projects and social banking such as Development Trusts Association Scotland and the Scottish Community Reinvestment Trust.

Ekopia currently has 220 members who have invested almost £400,000 in community initiatives.

(See Web References, page 171, for further reading.)

CHAPTER TEN

Governance

*The function of government, then, is not to make
and enforce laws as if life were reluctant to obey,
but to perceive that the real laws, the real power,
are in the very nature of life creating itself.*
— *PETER CADDY: Faces of Findhorn.*

Governance has to do with how decisions are made, and in Permaculture, how we make shared decisions in fellowship. This is all about fair sharing. We are not implying that this is an imposition of something from outside, but we look for the natural patterns that arise from the group, and facilitate these in a creative manner.

Peter Caddy called this "spiritual government". Often this calls for some individuals to take on leadership roles for periods of time.

Good governance promotes a sense of social stability and dynamism in community life; a foundation of safety and trust enables individuals to freely express themselves to the benefit of all.

Leadership and Power

The themes of leadership and power are inextricably linked. Often we have a negative view of leadership, as we associate it with the abuse of power. Sometimes we may have painful and difficult experiences of the abuse of power, which leads us to be suspicious and wary of anyone who claims to be, or acts as, a leader. The whole issue of leadership is fraught with challenges.

Coming from a background in the old paradigm, leadership was often linked to authority and responsibility. In the old hierarchical pyramid, with the king exercising his power from the top, this was often a rigid system, something that we can still discern echoes of in the British class system, and which still dominates the Indian social system with its caste divisions.

Inclusive Decision-Making Processes

The art of leading a circle of individuals where all voices are heard has to make a space for including everyone who is in the group. There is no doubt that there will be leaders, and authority and rank can often be discerned as attributes of individual character, experience, and the amount of time and effort that an individual has invested in the group.

Being aware of "Power Over" and "Power With" can often help as we strive to create "Power From Within". The word "Empowerment" has been a really useful addition to our vocabulary, and often very difficult to translate into other languages.

When a group can develop a culture of Empowerment, where each individual feels his or her power growing or developing out of themselves, this is an indication that a group is beginning to achieve a healthy decision-making process.

Conflict will inevitably arise. There is no group that does not experience conflict, but this does not necessarily condemn every group to failure. Conflict can be regarded as a sign or a symptom, and can be a useful indicator that a group needs to work on its own processes. Like any symptom, a course of the right treatment may well be all that is needed.

Conflicts can be seen as opportunities for growth, and as the Permaculture principle "turn a problem into a solution" indicates, be just what a group needs in order to upgrade its group dynamics.

In what follows, we have attempted to summarize some of the perspectives of a few experts on the questions of power and leadership. A deeper understanding of these issues will enable us to differentiate different forms of power, to notice and take action when power and leadership are being exercised in an oppressive way, and to welcome and support the leadership that is appropriate to our own particular situations.

Joanna Macy

Gaian Teacher Joanna Macy PhD, is a scholar of Buddhism, general systems theory, and deep ecology. A respected voice in the movements for peace, justice, and ecology, she interweaves her scholarship with five decades of activism. Joanna Macy differentiates two kinds of power, "Power Over" and "Power With". The first is oppressive, one or more people exercising power over others, who are then effectively disempowered. Depriving someone of their rights by, for example, putting them in a detention cell, is an exercise of force, not power.

Power With she also calls "Synergistic Power", which can be a process, or a verb. It happens through us. Power With is the capacity to act in ways that increase the sum total of conscious participation.

When we are in a relationship with a lover, partner or child and we see them developing their strengths and skills, joyfully daring to take risks then our sense of well-being is greater. At times like this, we know the power that consists of enhancing the power of others.

Power With, or synergistic power, summons us to develop our capacities for nurturing and empathy. It challenges men to be less competitive and dominant, and women to become more assertive, to participate more and take more responsibility.

In this context, and with this as our aim, lobbying for just laws, or removing from power those who misuse it, is not a struggle to "seize power" but is rather seeking to release it for decentralized use in self-governance.

Starhawk

Starhawk teaches Goddess religion and earth-based spirituality. She has taught the Permaculture Design Course in many countries, and is committed to global justice. Starhawk also recognizes both Power Over and Power With. The former is the power wielded by one person over another. The latter she defines as the influence we exert in a group of equals.

This may be top-down in a hierarchy, or broad-based in a collective. Decisions are made by those most affected by them and/or those who will carry them out. Key words here are control and decision-making.

Then she adds a third category, "Power From Within", which is the personal power we can evoke at any moment. This is influence, and may vary with different levels of skill, knowledge, imagination and experience of the individuals within the group. It is best when it is overt and acknowledged. When it is not acknowledged or is used negatively to institutionalize one person's position, it becomes destructive.

To empower its members a group must be structured in a way that serves liberation and understand how power in the group moves and flows.

There are two myths about leadership. One is that someone must be in charge to get something done, the other is that leadership is always oppressive. These myths are based on confusing Power With and Power Over. When Power With and Power From Within are used constructively they become synonymous with responsibility.

Starhawk uses the term, Responsive Leadership, to identify power or influence used to empower the group and its individuals. She sets out the following guidelines for this:

- Responsive leaders nurture others, train them up and see their own leadership as a temporary condition. They keep commitments, they respond, can accept criticism, and sense the underlying tone of the group. They take responsibility for decisions they make and are accountable to the group for them, while at the same time keeping lines of authority, power and decision-making clear and visible. Responsive leaders think first about the needs and interests of the group, and don't expect special benefits, attention or adulation, though they do expect support, nurturing and appreciation from the group.
- Responsive leaders do not judge or humiliate others, or determine what can and can't be said. They are self-disclosing by showing their vulnerability and feelings, and do not monopolize care-giving and caring. Most of all they make mistakes. If they do not make their share of mistakes they are not taking enough risks!

Arnold Mindell

When it comes to leadership and authority within group processes we inevitably come across the concept of "rank". It seems that some individuals have some quality that gives them more power than others. Indeed, power is not equally distributed among people, even within any group that randomly comes together.

Arnold Mindell is the founder of Process-Oriented Psychology (POP) and defines rank as "the sum of a person's privileges". He also says that it is *"a conscious or unconscious, social or personal ability or power arising from culture, community support, personal psychology and/or spiritual power"*. Whether you earned or inherited your rank, it organizes much of your communication behaviour.

All these considerations of power, authority, leadership and rank are not necessarily "good" or "bad", they are qualities or features of any group that comes together and that has to make decisions.

These qualities are all part of the invisible side of Permaculture, they are difficult to measure or quantify, but we recognize them, feel them, and often suffer from them because we don't give them sufficient conscious awareness.

Implicit in all this is the idea that a group is not just a random collection of individuals, but an organism in itself, a living entity.

As ecologies develop, grow and expand, they become more complex and more diverse. This is one of the basic laws of ecology and of life in general. The trend is towards more complexity, and this complexity and diversity in turn creates more stable and more resilient ecologies.

Human society can be seen as a highly complex organism, and when we factor in human consciousness, there is no doubt that we reach an even higher complexity. Any group process is an interaction between several human consciousnesses, and in Permaculture social design, we strive to create inclusive decision-making within groups.

Attunement

Craig spent a few years in retreat with some Tibetan friends learning something about meditation, observing his thoughts and feelings, the play of the mind upon the senses and the influence it had in colouring all of his perceptions. He found a new peace of mind and direction for his life. That direction led him to Findhorn where there was a strong meditative focus and it was there that he was introduced to the concept of attunement.

There were different applications to this process. One was very simple and spontaneous, by having a moment of silence before beginning any task. The group could be either sitting or standing, in a circle holding hands, each one

Gardeners at Findhorn beginning their work session with an attunement.

gently softening one's gaze and cultivating a sense of peace, just bringing yourself present to the moment.

Afterwards there is a brief check-in where everyone shares briefly how they are feeling. There would be a longer attunement lasting half a day once a week, always starting from that place of silence.

The second attunement process is using it in decision-making, from deciding where you live to ratifying the yearly budget. We would share all of the relevant details and factual information about the intention and when finally it seems that the group is moving to a level of consensus we would have the time of attunement.

A longer meditation would be led guiding the participants into a state of peace, then opening up to that collective field of intelligence that we had built by coming together as community.

Into this space of silence the question would be presented impartially, we would stay in this silence for a minimum of five minutes after which there would be a sharing. It's surprising what arises because it is not all clear and linear, it's more like collecting a series of images that form into tapestry. A pattern in Permaculture language – an overall design after having observed and listened to the weather, the landscape and the soil.

A very important part of bringing all this together into a consensus is the concept of being a loyal minority. This means listening to those who have opposing perceptions and honouring their points of view. All the voices are heard and valued.

Once that has taken place we ask: If you are disagreeing, will you be a loyal minority and allow the collective to move ahead? Being a spiritual community each one learning to surrender their position and support others is a primary lesson.

Being in a Permaculture garden and learning to surrender your position as the dominant Gardener is the primary lesson. Everything is gardening.

"We are all storytellers, mythmakers: our lives, our thoughts, feelings, dreams, desires and self-images are tales that we project to the world. Like the stories that ancient men and women told around campfires and in sacred places, our myths give definition, meaning, order and significance to our personal realities.

Cultures are like stories, too. They are tales told by some part of the humanity about what it means to be human, to live on this Earth, to strive, to rejoice, to feel pain, to sorrow, to be born, to die, to triumph and to transcend."

— *Faces of Findhorn, Findhorn Publications, 1980.*

Governance at Findhorn

The Findhorn Community began with a very clear leadership, a leadership committed to inner listening and following that still small voice within. The founders were very clear that the guidance they received was from a wider sense of perception beyond the purely human.

Eileen called it God, God in the sense of a unified field in which all creation rests. Listening to one's heart, to nature and the potential of humanity committed to living in harmony with one another and with all the other communities of life.

Dorothy Maclean was both surprised and delighted that through this process of inner listening she was able to contact the Angelic or Devic energies that infuse the nature kingdoms, enhancing the manifestation of life and the beauty that we all perceive.

The Devas were very clear that if we humans would partnership with them then this planet would be healed. We call it Co-creation with nature.

Just as Permaculture begins with Observation and Listening, we began listening to the earth beneath us, the sky above us, and the wind and the rain. Working with nature and the nature of oneself, allowing the garden to garden.

Ecovillage Experience Week participants join hands in the centre as a symbol of co-operation, connection and equality in groups.

The beauty of these experiments was that this inner voice told Eileen Caddy to cease being the sole voice guiding Peter and the community, and that everyone should get their own inner guidance and direction. All of the early founders and future leaders of the community have released their authority and power, stepping aside allowing others to express their unique alignment with the creation.

There was an explosion of creativity: gardeners, artists, musicians, dancers, potters, painters, storytellers, builders, cooks and bottle washers, not to mention the managers, the accountants, the engineers and the mothers and babies with schools to follow. None of this was really planned. It was just the plan of love and light unfolding.

❦

This allowed the community to evolve, adapt and change, absorbing new ideas while releasing the more hierarchical structures of the early days. The centralized Community Core Group devolved, and a community of communities and social enterprises began to spring up.

Even the local town joined the Transition Towns movement, inspired by Permaculture. This was a very natural organic evolution with the physical and metaphysical in partnership, strengthening and supporting the diversity of our local bioregion.

As the community grew in complexity our greatest challenge was personal communication and governance. There was a need to develop the psyche, not just the soul. Working with the mind and emotions, integrating them into the heart, and expressing healthy human relationships. Singing and dancing had brought us a long way, but we needed to go deeper, so we began to use many of the emerging psychological techniques available.

Jung was already accepted and Psycho-Synthesis was also explored. Co-counselling was practised along with EST (Erhart Seminar Training). By the mid-1980s we were experimenting with Holotropic Breath work, Appreciative Enquiry, Non-Violent Communication, the Forum, and today, Sociocracy is being adopted by different groups.

Comparing it to a thriving Permaculture garden there was an immense diversity, a multitude of relationships and expressions. The seasons and the cycles of nature informed the rhythm and life of the community.

PERSONAL STORY · LYNDALL PARRIS

My way to Narara Ecovillage

FOR ME THE LEARNINGS from the journey of founding an Ecovillage have been through and with Spirit —the delightful and astounding discovery that with patience, perseverance, and persistence, my dream of life having a different story could be realized. That events could unfold not in my planned time frame, but in divine time which turned out to be better, given all aspects of my life.

I discovered after setting a vision and direction for "the best" future, that if I listened, responded, trusted and followed up on the serendipity of what actually unfolded, the results were either gobsmacking and/or way better than what I envisaged.

Initially, I struggled with letting go of the conventional western planning wisdom of adhering to a formulated plan then, slowly I began allowing for other possibilities to arise. There was a double benefit. Often and surprisingly, I found that when I was able to surrender control, needing to activate every situation and being the pivot, I found freedom and space for the next thing that was juicing me up or calling for my attention and, found that what ensued was often beyond my dreams.

Gracefully, life directed me, if I only let it! By taking me out of the country and/or ensuring my preoccupation with something else, other people rose to deal with a particular situation or issue.

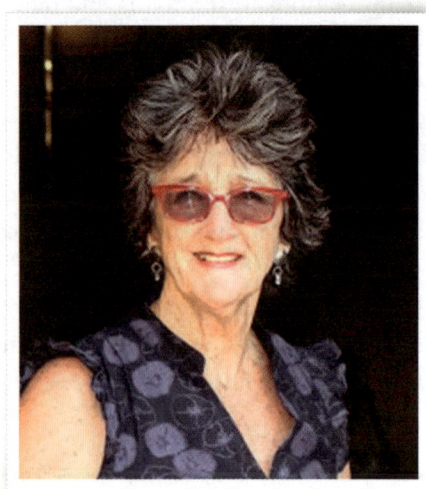

Lyndall Parris

I was enthralled to observe that progress didn't need my struggle and started wondering... could life actually be easy? That emptying myself of fear, striving and forcing in a particular direction, seemed to pave the way for more joy and progress in an unimagined direction, beyond my vision and dreams – an outcome and future that was surprisingly better than I ever could have imagined.

NOTE: *Lyndall Parris is founder and Community Director of Narara Ecovillage Co-operative Ltd. She lives and works in Australia.*

PART FOUR

Bringing It All Together

We can see the world and our place in it through the lens of ecology. Ecology is, after all, simply the relationships among organisms and their environment.

— *FRANCES MOORE LAPPÉ*

Most of us are familiar with the extinction of the dinosaurs about 60 million years ago. What exactly triggered this is not entirely clear, though many geologists agree that a giant asteroid impact was involved.

What everyone seems to agree upon is that the preceding era is known as the Era of Dinosaurs, and the succeeding one, the Era of Mammals. At the end of the Era of the Dinosaurs, small furry creatures that fed their young with milk for the first few weeks of their lives, and that regulated their body heat themselves, appeared.

After the dinosaurs disappeared, it was these creatures, the mammals, that eventually took over the planet. If the theory of evolution is correct, we are their descendants.

More recent research into the long history of our planet reveals that there were several great extinctions in the past; every 100 million years or less. Most researchers agree that the one already mentioned was the fifth extinction, and that today we are beginning another one, the sixth extinction.

It seems that there is a general and slow rate of species extinction, more or less balanced by the appearance of new species. Over the last two to three centuries, the rate of species extinction has increased well beyond this background rate, and we are looking at increasing numbers of species becoming extinct over the next century or two, if present rates are to continue.

Some researchers are estimating that species are disappearing at the rate of 150 PER DAY!

One pattern that seems to recur throughout these great extinctions is the replacement of one dominant life system by a more complex one. We see this clearly in the changeover from the reptile dinosaurs to the heat-generating mammals. Previous extinctions saw the emergence of life forms on land, and increasing complexity in plant life. What might our extinction herald as the next, more complex life form?

We have seen a rapid development of human consciousness over the last few millennia. Ten thousand years ago we were largely composed of small bands of humans who moved nomadically across the landscapes we inhabited, collecting our food directly from nature's bounty.

Around 4,000 years ago we began some hesitant steps to inventing writing, and about 2, 000 years ago we were collecting libraries containing vast amounts of information.

Around that time the major religious and philosophical ideas were laid down, and are still the foundations of most of our thinking today.

Could it be that the next, more complex, life form would be some form of group consciousness? If so, might it not require new forms of thinking? Is this what the new paradigm is really all about?

As Permaculturalists, we try to see the solution within the problem, the future within the challenge. If we are entering another period of extinction, it could sound pretty much of a drag. After all, who wants to see life dying all around? However, if this is what is needed to usher in the next major evolutionary leap, how exciting to be part of it!

Permaculture Design is about thinking habits, and finding new and better ones, habits that are relevant to the ecology of the planet we find ourselves on. In which case we should be looking for our partners. None of us within the Permaculture family should be so arrogant as to believe that Permaculture is the ONLY solution.

We are part of a much bigger picture, a mass movement of people who are intent on building a new and better culture, who are looking for ecological compatibility, for human rights, for peace and justice and generally for a better world.

Not just for us humans, but for all the creatures that we share our planet with.

The last two chapters in this book are exactly about that. About how to combine all the disparate elements that we have covered in the previous chapters, and how to locate our partners in building a better world for the future.

In Permaculture we like to talk about hands-on design, but we have seen how there is a big need for us to include our hearts. We need hearts-on design. We need to include the whole person in the design process, and we have seen that the spiritual dimension is one that is increasingly being recognized both by science and by people generally.

CHAPTER ELEVEN

Design Hands-On, Hearts-On

When we get right down to it, all that is needed is a
change of mind, and minds can change very quickly.
It is a new awareness, rather than any technological fix,
that will ultimately set us upon the right course.
— *ALBERT BATES, Climate in Crisis.*

We Are All Designers

Everyone is a designer, planning events in your lives, and shaping your surroundings. Design is not some esoteric art reserved only for a small minority of the educationally initiated, but a skill we learn from living our lives. Permaculture will awaken the awareness of this skill.

Our job as facilitators is to remind you of your skills, talents and knowledge. In this sense it's important to understand that design is not reserved for a professional time and place, but an activity that happens spontaneously whenever we think about space and time.

In *The Greening of America*, Charles Reich points out that "consciousness plays a key role in the shaping of society". When we consider that Permaculture is a design tool, which is just another way of saying that it's about thinking with both the heart, mind and hand, we appreciate how important this is in shaping society.

By anchoring Permaculture firmly in the new paradigm, we can actually begin creating the infrastructure of that paradigm on the ground in the shape of buildings, farms, gardens and social structures.

The Magic of Design

When we design things in this world, we often start with a thought, an idea. This does not exist in the physical sense, though it may have an existence as a mental picture. We can share this with others, and create a group idea. This might be something quite specific, a mulched vegetable garden, a herb spiral or a solar collector.

IDEA

DESIGN

OBJECT

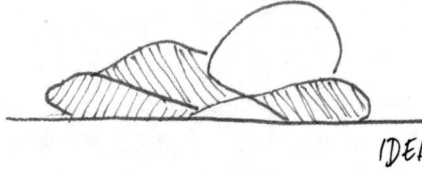

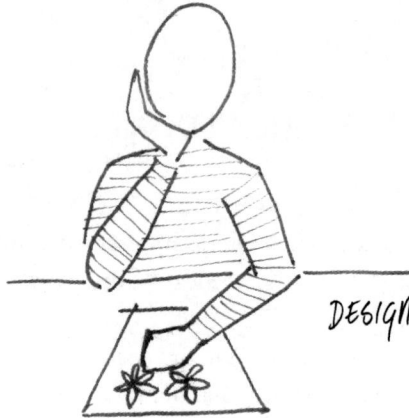

The magic of design

We can move a step closer to the material world by drawing it, sketching it out on paper, even marking it out on the ground. At some point we will need to actually get out tools and start work on the material construction, and at this point a dialogue will begin, testing our ideas in the physical world, bending matter to our design.

Small, unforeseen problems will arise all the time, and our design will modify itself as we go along. Finally the finished product will appear and exist in the world, though of course anything that exists over time will change, need modification and maintenance, requiring further dialogue with the material as we adjust and change.

This process consists of creating something out of nothing. The thought that arises has no physical existence in the material world, and gradually creates a new object, through the work of our hands. Design is much more than just planning a thing or an event, it is transforming a thought into an object. It is a bridge between the world as an idea and the world as material.

In Permaculture, not only do we work on making this process easier, but we also make it conscious. We should be aware of our capacities for doing design, and aware of how amazing this skill is. For most non-human creatures, this is a process governed by instincts, habits and traditions.

However amazing a termite's tower or a bower bird's mating area might be, neither the termite nor the bower bird has any capacity for designing something else, or even making major modifications to their design. They are trapped in a habit, albeit a wonderful one. We humans seem to be unique in our capacity to design things that no one has ever thought of before.

Permaculture takes this capacity and links it in with the ecology of the planet. This is a linkage that has been forgotten, neglected or consciously done away with over the last few hundred years of our western, materialist world-view.

A New Way of Thinking

Frances Moore Lappé, in her book *Ecomind*, writes:

> *"We can see the world and our place in it through the lens of ecology. Ecology is, after all, simply the relationships among organisms and their environment."*

Using this idea, she cuts through the barriers we have developed that stop us from making changes. By changing the way we think, she shows that there are many good things already happening out there in the world, and that material change is possible by changing the way we think.

Again, another reminder that it's the invisible, the power of thought, that is the key to change. All the recipes, all the technology and the know-how, are already in place, we just have to start using them.

The challenge today is that most of the solutions offered to us by the mainstream are based on the thinking of the old reductionist materialist paradigm. The institutions that operate today are mostly cast in the forms of the past. The issues we are facing, be they climate change, economic collapse, social unrest, militarism or a host of others, are all interlinked, so that solutions aimed at ameliorating one challenge often cause other, new problems down the line.

The solutions are not technical, but require a new way of thinking, thinking like the planet. Albert Bates calls them *"problems of justice, fairness and responsibility"*. What we need is to work on our awareness and consciousness and not limit ourselves only to technical solutions.

As he says in our opening quote, *"... all that (cf. p.151) what is needed is a change of mind..."* That is exactly what Permaculture is about, changing our minds.

Linking to the Mystics

We have seen how many of the insights of modern science responding to the new paradigm involve both matter and mind, both material and immaterial. An enormous opening has been created, allowing things that cannot be measured materially to become serious considerations, worthy of scientific research.

Theodore Roszac welcomes these *"transactional possibilities between mind and matter, the human and non-human"*. Many of these insights reflect thinking that has been handed down to us from mystical traditions, both Western and Oriental. Images of nature are back in fashion.

Many of these ancient traditions have drawn upon deep experiences inspired by nature. Within our Western religious traditions, the roots of Judaism can be said to be founded upon the meeting between Moses and God deep in the Sinai Desert. Christianity, which grew out of Judaism, is centred upon the teachings of Jesus Christ, who began his ministry by fasting in the Judean Desert for 40 days. Mohammed received the Koran in a cave in the desert of today's Saudi Arabia. All these spiritual traditions are rich in references to nature, and include mystical teachings that are nature-based.

Myth and ritual have been the ways these teachings have been handed down over the centuries, and some of these rituals are of value for us today. Many belief systems have a form of praying before meals, often involving blessing the food.

Today we would do well to consider how our food was grown and produced, and send a thought of gratefulness to all those people who have helped that food find its way to our table. This is not religious mumbo jumbo, but a way of expanding our awareness about what we eat, and avoiding the old saying about modern children thinking that milk comes from supermarkets.

If we can envisage that we live in an intelligent ecology here on this planet, which itself may well be a living organism, according to James Lovelock and Lynn Margulis, how might we expect this organism to warn us that we are mistreating it?

Clearly we are being told in no uncertain terms that enough is enough. With the burning of carbon now irrefutably connected to global climate change, the message could not be clearer: "Burn less!", or better still, "Use no fossil fuels!"

Another way the planet might tell us would be to raise the conscience of more and more individuals. That might sound far-fetched, but it's exactly what researchers are finding.

Paul Hawken talks of multi-millions of people engaged in human rights, peace and justice, and environmental activism. These are largely conscience-driven activities. People don't get rich lobbying for less pollution and more organic agriculture.

The design that we need for taking us into the future will have to be expanded to include all aspects of the human being, all aspects of the natural ecology, and combine the thinking of the head, the feelings of the heart and the will-power that we exercise through our hands.

We need to bring it all together.

The Development of Findhorn

The founders of the Findhorn Community never intended to start building a community when they moved their caravan onto the Findhorn Bay Caravan site and nestled it amongst the sand dunes alongside a rubbish dump.
They were three adults and three young boys living in a very confined space that would be their home for the next eight years. Peter Caddy would say it was here that they began to learn the lessons of living together in the community.

There was a major cohesive factor holding them together and that was their inner spiritual practice of listening to the still small voice within and following its direction. There were no master plans or designs. They did not even own the land that they were beginning to transform into the fabled Findhorn Gardens.

There was a strong commitment to meditate daily and connect with the overlighting soul of humanity and the plan of love and light. It was from this place that simple directions on what to do each day were followed. Eileen Caddy was even told to go down to the public toilets early each morning if she needed peace and quiet. Through this Eileen underwent a disciplined spiritual initiation.

They were unemployed and dependent on a tiny State benefit, so they began to grow some of their own food on the barren windswept sand dunes, and composting became a major task in building a healthy soil structure. Peter, who was the major gardener, had the insight to ask Dorothy Maclean to contact the life-force permeating the natural worlds and in particular that of the vegetables he was growing.

Dorothy was both surprised and delighted by what she received when tuning into a particular species. She named them the Devas. They too were delighted that humans were willing to communicate with them. It was this connection that gave birth to Findhorn's work with the nature kingdoms, conscious co-creation with nature.

It was a very natural organic growth, one thing leading to another. People were attracted by the joy, laughter and openness of spirit; by the beauty of the gardens, and the abundance of a simple holistic lifestyle. As the gardens grew so did the infrastructure, it was easy just to add on another caravan or turn a double garage into a sanctuary.

A great deal of time was given over to developing tools of communication between people. Songs, dances, games, storytelling, attunements and meditations were used to deepen that sense of community. We began to grow people, working with the same principles of inner listening and co-creation.

Craig Gibsone's artistic representation
of Spirits of Nature.

Garden Cottage

IT'S AMAZING how many common phrases are actually deeply perceptive. *Home is where the heart is* sits at the centre of this observation. It's just a little (true) tale about how I became connected with both permaculture and Findhorn one summer's night in the early 1980s.

I had travelled to stay with my friend Jo Steranka near Lincoln (England) from my then home in London. We were green party activists together (indeed, responsible for ensuring The Ecology Party was renamed the Green Party – all about accessibility). She went out for the evening to attend some local meeting and left me with a flagon of pea pod wine and her library. I've always enjoyed other people's books.

A few years later I made pea pod wine myself and it was just as bad as Jo's. But the books were great. I ended up with two, bouncing backwards and forwards between them: *The Findhorn Garden* (in the original black and white version) and an original copy of *Permaculture One*. This latter was David Holmgren and Bill Mollison's proposition for the theory of permaculture.

The original edition was home-published on what could have been recycled toilet paper with some very basic drawings of lollipop trees which my five year old children could have surpassed. All kinds of other stuff made it a very basic effort. The Findhorn Garden (on the other hand) was this magical experience. Amazing photographs of plants in the early garden… Dorothy's experience of talking with the plant devas.

As I flitted between the two texts one thing became apparent. The attractions of the Findhorn Garden seemed remote and unachievable. Permaculture One (however inferior as a production) bound together all the things I really cared about – sustainable food production, renewable energy, woodland integrated into the landscape, sustainable housing etc., etc., in such a way that it seemed do-able. Here was a vision I could understand and create for myself.

Somewhere after this I got together with Nancy and we decided that Green Politics (telling people there was a better way) should give way to green living (doing it) and we espoused permaculture as how we would consciously design what we did. We moved to Scotland.

Various ups and downs (failing to create an intentional community – deciding the village we lived in was such anyway) have seen us, twenty-five years later, living in the oldest forest garden in the UK. This garden is one fifth of an acre, that's one tenth of a hectare and can produce a metric tonne of food every year as well as producing all our firewood and hosting a plant nursery.

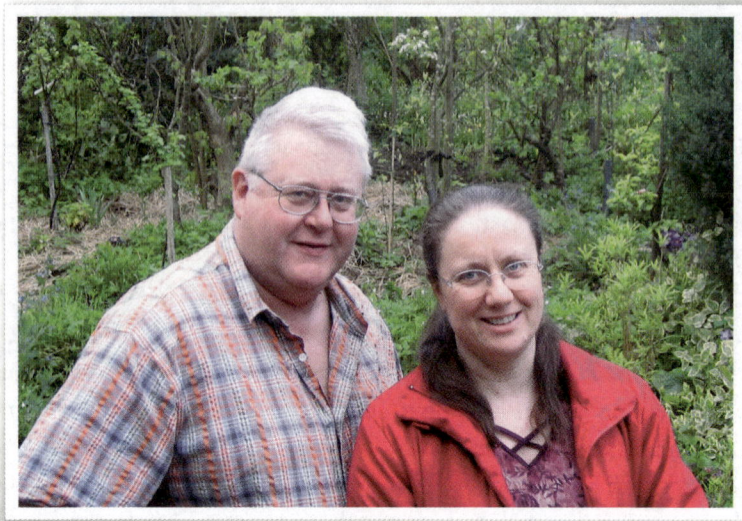

Graham and Nancy Bell

In itself it is a hugely spiritual experience. Sharing it with others adds to the dimension. And oh yes… the plants do talk to me, now I can hear them. Bill Mollison once berated Biodynamics to me. I said, "It's just homeopathy for the landscape." He said, "You don't believe in fairies do you?"

Cottage garden

I'm not sure. But I know that Bill, like me, believes in the spiritual necessities of life. He just has an Australian way of expressing it. And the introduction to this book suggests we always had three ethics to permaculture. Yes and no: actually those came out of David Holmgren's years away, proving it worked as a design system. He had learned that communicating snappily is useful.

If there isn't soul in it, it's not permaculture. A deep understanding and love of nature drives everything we do. As a family we could have done much better (financially) buying a property in Edinburgh all those years ago. But we weren't investing in property. We were creating a home.

Home *is* where the heart is. We're open to visitors: see the website for open days or make a direct contact for a personal appointment.

(See Web References, page 171, for further details.)

CHAPTER TWELVE

Permaculture in Partnership

The challenge of the future is to reach out to embrace all groups
that are working in a way that benefits humanity, regardless of
labels. That's where courage comes in – to really step out and be
open to people on different paths who may even have initially
hostile or critical attitudes to what you are doing.
— HELEN *in Faces of Findhorn, Findhorn Publications, 1980.*

From Traumaculture to Permaculture

We have much to learn from the old established religious traditions. Not just their content, but also from the way they present ideas and ways of dealing with life and its problems. From Buddhism we have the Noble Eightfold Path, and we would like to present something similar in Permaculture; "The Eightfold path of Permaculture", below:

Global Crisis

Permaculture did not arise in a vacuum, but as a response to some of the complicated and interlinked problems that we face on this planet, problems which seemed serious enough in the 1970s to inspire Mollison and Holmgren to look for solutions, and which seem to have become more serious over the intervening decades.

In addition to the social conflicts and the recurring economic crises, we are facing global warming and peak everything; peak oil, peak metals, peak water, you name it, there'll be a shortage coming your way soon. These are symptoms that something is wrong, and just this shift in thinking already gives us a positive boost.

Design as a Solution

Permaculture tries not to dwell on the negative aspects, but chooses design as our way out of problems, indeed, turning problems into challenges and solutions, finding the answer within the question.

We see that the systems we have created in order to grow our food, build our houses, manage our finances and distribute the things we need are not compatible with a sustainable future on this planet. We choose design to create our future.

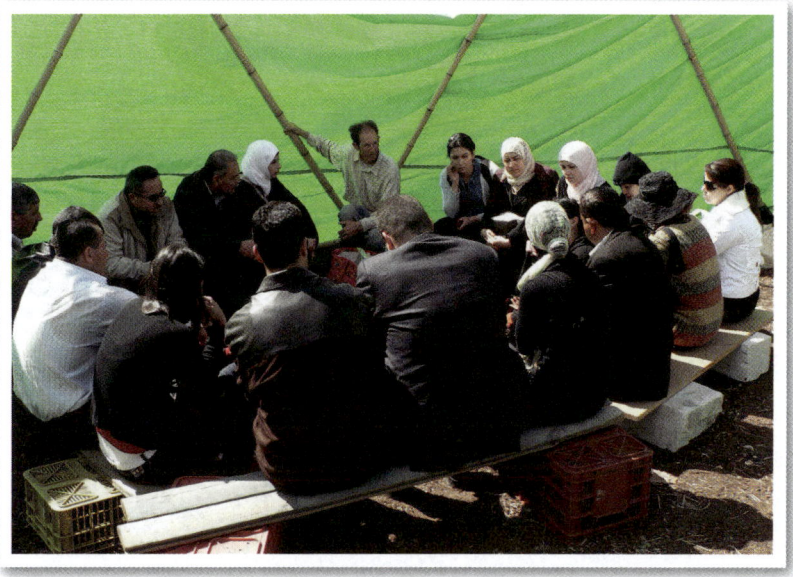

Design as a solution: a Permaculture course for Palestinians
held in Israel in 2008.

Systems that support Humans

The systems we create are there to support us and all life. It's clearly insane to think that the western capitalist, corporate economic system is somehow ordained by either God or laws of nature and is there to be served by us.

We are not servants of the global food distribution system. It is there to make sure that food gets distributed from the producer to the consumer. We should be the boss. We need practical solutions and strategies for improving existing systems.

Models in Nature

We live on a planet with a well functioning ecological system, and Permaculture consciously looks to that system for models to use in our designs. We trust nature, we learn from nature and we try to copy nature. This is the central concept in Permaculture that we come back to at every turn.

Personal Responsibility

Everyone can do something. One of the simple precepts of Permaculture is not to try to do something that you can't do. Choose changes that you can follow through. In this way you will achieve a positive feeling of successful achievement, which will inspire you to do other things, at the same time as inspiring other people by your example. We don't give up hope but go from success to success.

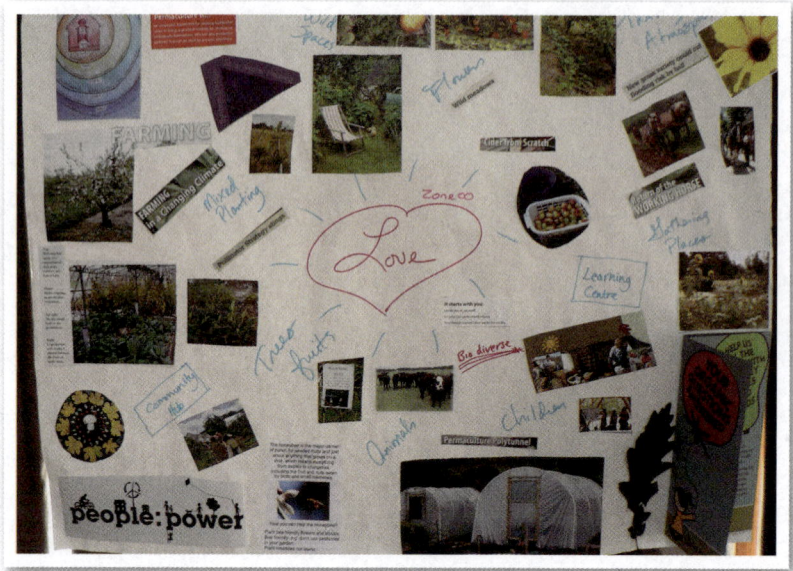

Love is at the centre.

Practical Initiatives

Permaculture is essentially a practical way of dealing with the future. We work with our hands. We garden, farm, build and assemble. We create systems, be they anchored in the material world, such as gardens and houses, or in the social arena of associations, education or business.

We work with other people, finding partners and forging alliances. We should be thinking globally, but we are usually acting locally.

Global Networking

Permaculture is a network rather than a hierarchical organization where ideas and rules flow down from a top position dominated by a small handful of people. The basis is local or national groups, who tend to meet together as regional groups at more or less regular intervals.

There is scarcely a country in the world where you will not find either Permaculture, Ecovillage or Transition Town groups. Every few years there are international conferences or convergences, called the latter because that's exactly what they are, informal meetings between people who practice Permaculture in different ways.

The advances in internet-based information exchange over the last two decades mean that internationally the Permaculture network is highly integrated. People travel as never before, Permaculture teachers and designers no less. People really know each other or of each other, and new information and new linkages are flowing across the web continuously.

Within minutes of hearing about a new technique or a new technology, we can assemble enough material about it to understand it. Email and skype means that we can keep in touch over distances instantly and easily, and these are readily used by the Permaculture network. Courses can be delivered online, which is a useful way of imparting information and some skills, though on-line courses have the disadvantage that a group is not together physically as much as on the usual 14-day foundation course, so the social and group dynamics cannot be explored in as much depth.

Solutions

All these steps lead us to solutions. In fact, each one is a minor solution in itself, and builds upon the last step. These solutions are both in the realm of ideas, ways of thinking about the world, and in the material realm when we apply techniques such as mulch gardening or community-supported agriculture. They engage us personally and make activists of us, and inevitably they lead to community.

This is the cutting edge of Permaculture, the groups of people who actively use Permaculture as an everyday tool in some way, getting themselves together. This gives an opportunity to share, to listen, to learn, and to construct larger systems such as groups of courses, networks of designers at work in supplying human needs.

In many ways, Permaculture leads us to community, but a new type of community, where part of the social glue holding us together is a shift in the way we perceive and think about the world.

Shift in Consciousness

Joanna Macy and Chris Johnstone, writing in *The Song of the Earth*, define three steps or dimensions as reference points in what they call The Great Turning. The first they call Holding Actions, attempts to limit the damage caused by the actions taken by those who still are anchored in the old reductionist materialist thinking: the pollution, the climate change, the social and economic damage.

The world is full of organizations working on this, organizations that seem to be growing, proliferating and becoming better organized as time goes by.

The second is creating Life-sustaining Systems and Practices. Here we are setting up alternatives or complementary systems that begin to create a new culture and a new civilization. Permaculture is a supremely well-suited tool for just this, as long as it is anchored in the thinking of the new paradigm.

Two movements that have emerged out of Permaculture spring to mind straight away, the Transition Towns movement, and the Global Ecovillage Network. In the standard Permaculture Design Course (PDC) we teach a whole host of related strategies, including Community Supported Agriculture, Local Exchange Trading Systems, Bioregional Organization, ecological house building and many more. These are all our closest partners.

Macy and Johnstone go on to identify yet another dimension that characterizes The Great Turning, that they call The Shift in Consciousness. This is essentially the new paradigm by yet another name. A new way of looking at the world, which they also call "the beautiful convergence of science and spirituality".

We have returned to this theme throughout this book. Our aim has been to show how Permaculture needs to be enriched by this new thinking. If it is not, Permaculture will make itself irrelevant in the future.

Cultural Creatives

Writing in 2000 Paul Ray and Sherry Anderson define just over 50 million Cultural Creatives in the USA. They were identifying groups and individuals who were working to improve or create the things that go to make up our world, covering virtually every aspect of human activity.

Looking at the mix of people and groups that make up these Cultural Creatives, they find a significant number of religious and spiritual groups, including traditional religious Christians, Evangelicals, Catholics and Episcopalians, moving towards

> *"psychological counselling, meditation and concern for the inner life, downplaying an exclusive emphasis on personal salvation".*

They went on to identify two different levels of cultural creativity, with what they called the "Core Group" composed of nearly half of the 50 million Cultural Creatives. The characteristics of the Core Group were that individuals within it strongly valued personal growth and spirituality and that they were the creative leading edge of the subculture.

These are the people we in the Permaculture movement need to forge alliances with and work together with. In 2014 Jan had a series of meetings with a Hindu-inspired meditation and retreat centre in Norway. At the initial meeting, after explaining what Permaculture was, one of the management group of the place exclaimed:

"We are talking the same language! We just don't know how to build these things, can you help us?"

During the following year the centre invited a number of Permaculture experts to help them build composting toilets, a herb spiral, vegetable beds and a greenhouse. While still practising Vedic Art, Sufi Healing and meditation retreats, they are incorporating the technologies that Permaculture can offer and helping to weave a rich tapestry for a new culture.

Centres of Light

I think that we are living in the most exciting period of history, a time of great change and transformation. How quickly this transformation comes about depends on how all of us experience it in our lives; how much love and light we can embody; how well we form together in groups and families to live in love and harmony.

Centres of Light are emerging throughout the world as catalysts and points of stability, and the network of Light is growing stronger as people move between these centres.

Times of political, social and economic turmoil are ahead, and I see that in coming years the world will need centres of stability, of love and light, balance and synthesis. It is important that these centres be linked up and that we each find that synthesis within ourselves.

— *PETER CADDY in* Faces of Findhorn, Findhorn Publications, 1980.

Those early metaphors of communities being called centres of light and that there was a network of light all over the planet, was the only way to explain what we felt we were creating. Light illuminated the heart and the soul.

As things became more physical and buildings appeared, gardens grew and businesses flourished, we at Findhorn became a village. We called ourselves a planetary village because there was a network of communities forming around the planet.

Later that network of communities began to call itself the Global Ecovillage Network. GEN was born. The network of light took physical form, quietly growing like a mycelium being nurtured by the creative forces of nature. Earth my body, Water my blood, Air my breath and Fire my spirit.

There was a beauty to this unfolding pattern and all its diversity of expression. Each centre had its own unique identity, and all were committed to creating a sustainable future for the coming generations of all species. They are the laboratories for learning the skills of living in harmony on this beautiful blue planet whirling through space. Centres of light, living together in love and harmony.

Paul Hawken, in researching the millions of organizations that are engaged in cultural creativity (his definitions are very close to those used by Paul Ray and Sherry Anderson), compares them to the body's immune system. Just like our own immune system responds to change in our body, the Cultural Creatives are responding to signals that the planet is giving us.

These are the rising global temperatures, the more chaotic weather events, and economic collapse leading to stressed social situations. Permaculture offers us a host of techniques to deal with these, and we see that where they are implemented, real positive change begins to occur.

This analysis of Hawken's is based on the idea of the planet being a living organism, often called the Gaia Theory.

James Lovelock and Lynn Margulis coined the Gaia Theory in the early 1970s, posing an idea that the Earth was displaying all the characteristics of a living organism. In *The Ages of Gaia,* Lovelock states that: *"Gaia is a religious as well as a scientific concept."* He calls theology a kind of science, but one with no place for creeds and dogmas, and goes on to show how the life of a natural philosopher and scientist can be deeply religious.

Good science rooted in a curiosity about the natural world can be very deep and infused with a loving relationship between humanity and nature.

The Future of Permaculture

In his book *Permaculture – Principles and Pathways Beyond Sustainability*, published in 2002, David Holmgren identifies three waves of environmental development over the period that Permaculture has been developing.

The first was when Permaculture initially emerged, after the Club of Rome report and the oil crises of the early 1970s. The second was in the late 1980s when awareness of the greenhouse gas effect became established, and Permaculture experienced a rapid growth and consolidation immediately after this.

The third wave he identifies as the turn of the century, and he regards his book as his contribution to this third growth spurt in Permaculture.

Jan certainly belongs to that third wave. He first started teaching Permaculture in the late 1990s and gained his Diploma in 2006. He has seen the steady growth of both the Global Ecovillage Network, and the Transition Towns initiatives, both of which emerged from Permaculture.

He has taught in several countries and watched new emerging national Permaculture networks. As Permaculture expands and develops, it has come into contact with many other similar ideas and movements, something that enriches Permaculture, but at the same time can cause confusion.

How much can we pull in from other ideas and incorporate into Permaculture? Will we water it down to such an extent that it becomes transparent and unrecognizable? Who do we want as partners, and who do we not want to be associated with?

Many people who first hear about Permaculture seem to think that it's just a better way to grow carrots. We have often come across this, and it's one of the first things we try to put right. Permaculture is a design system, it's a way of thinking that can be used for most things, and it's really good for planning houses, gardens and farms.

Expanding to include all forms of human endeavour is a really exciting exercise, and makes Permaculture much more relevant and much more universal. But of course Permaculture has its fundamentalists, just like every other way of thinking.

Not so long ago we came across people who defined themselves as "Mollisonian Permaculturalists", implying that this was the true version, and that it shouldn't be diluted by other ways of thinking. Maybe we will eventually have different branches of the subject, "Holmgrennian"? "Lawtonian"?

There has been an on-going debate about spirituality within Permaculture for some time. Several years ago there was a serious confrontation between those who thought that vegetarianism was against the ethos of Permaculture and those who chose not to eat meat. This occasionally surfaces even today.

In the early days there were strong sentiments against keeping dogs and cats as pets, but this has not been an issue for some time.

Permaculture itself changes slowly over the years, which is surely a sign of healthy life. Something that does not change becomes rigid and fossilized.

One of the more interesting developments in recent years is the emergence of "People-centred" Permaculture, especially with the book *People and Permaculture* published by Looby Macnamara in 2012. This focus upon Zone Zero, our own inner workings, the way we work together as human groups, and using the Permaculture principles as guides here, is a really exciting and fruitful expansion.

This book you are reading right now is a contribution to this debate about what Permaculture is and is not.

We have seen how the cutting edge of modern science is opening up new ways of seeing the world, or maybe reinforcing ancient ones. This new paradigm is exactly the kind of thinking that we need in order to solve the problems that are now confronting us. In many ways we have reached the end of a certain kind of thinking: the materialist reductionist way of regarding life and the cosmos.

We have seen how this new thinking will permeate every field of human endeavour, the way we farm our food, build our houses, and supply ourselves with water and energy. This thinking will come to affect how we treat each other, govern ourselves and allocate resources.

Permaculture, with its comprehensive Permaculture Design Course, is admirably suited to help each one of us see the connections between the different parts and how they affect each other. Each one of us can then design our way of living, more or less together with others, in families, in communities and in any other groupings we can think of. In this way we can build a future that does not damage the planet or ourselves.

Most of the technical details we teach in Permaculture are not new or even that radical, they are mostly tried and tested techniques based on either traditional ways, or on detailed observation. The way we put things together may be surprising to those who are still used to dividing the world up into pieces and putting them into different compartments. Permaculture looks for the hidden connections, the invisible aspects of things and their relationships. These hidden details give us insights and ideas, inspirations and discoveries, about the world and also about ourselves.

Permaculture is a good tool chest of techniques, but needs to be much more than that. It has to be a source of enlightenment, of self-knowledge, like the Biodynamic farmer using agriculture to grow as a person, develop his or her personality, become a better person. It would be a shame if Permaculture were to be only a set of material techniques, only a way of fixing details that are not working.

After four decades of development, now is the time for Permaculture to mature, to become an adult, to find its place in the world. As the new paradigm gradually seeps through into our way of thinking, Permaculture is the right set of tools, in the right place, at the right time.

We hope that this book will help Permaculture along its way, will seek out partners that we can build a better world together with, and will contribute to a new and more holistic way of looking at the world and at ourselves.

Bibliography

Alexander, Christopher. *A Pattern Language*. Oxford University Press, UK, 1977.

——. *The Timeless Way of Building*. Oxford University Press, UK, 1979.

Bates, Albert. *Climate in Crisis*. The Book Publishing Company, USA, 1990.

Budd, Christopher Houghton, ed. **Rudolf Steiner** – *Economist*. New Economy Publications, UK, 1996.

Capra, Fritjof. *The Turning Point*. Wildwood House,UK, 1982.

Coats, Callum. *Living Energies*. Gateway Books, UK, 1996.

Day, Christopher. *Places of the Soul*. Aquarian/Thorsons, UK, 1990.

Disch, Robert, ed. *The Ecological Conscience*. Prentice Hall, USA, 1970.

Eddington, Sir Arthur. *The Philosophy of Physical Science*. Cambridge University Press, UK, 1939.

Fukuoka, Masanobu. *The One-Straw Revolution*. Rodale Press, USA, 1978.

Girardet, Herbert and Mendonca, Miguel. *A Renewable World, Energy, Ecology Equality*. Green Books, UK, 2009.

Griffiths, Bede. *Return to the Centre*. Harper Collins, USA, 1976.

——. *A New Vision of Reality*. Harper Collins, USA, 1989.

——. *Universal Wisdom*. Harper Collins, USA, 1994.

Hageneder, Fred. *The Spirit of Trees*. Floris Books, UK, 2000.

Hargittai, Istvan and Magdolna. *Symmetry – A Unifying Concept*. Shelter Publications, USA, 1994.

Harland, Maddy and Keepin, Will, eds. *The Song of the Earth*. Permanent Publications, UK, 2012.

Hawken, Paul. *Blessed Unrest*. Penguin, UK, 2007.

Higgins, Ronald. *The Seventh Enemy*. Hodder and Stoughten, UK, 1982.

Holmgren, David. *Permaculture – Principles and Pathways Beyond Sustainability*. Holmgren Design Services, Australia, 2002.

Hyams, Edward. *Soil and Civilization*. John Murray, UK, 1976.

Jeans, Sir James. *The Mysterious Universe*. Penguin, UK, 1937.

Kabat-Zinn, Jon. *Wherever You Go There You Are*. Hyperion, USA, 1994.

Koestler, Arthur. *The Yogi and the Commissar*. Collier Books, USA, 1961.

——. *The Sleepwalkers*. Penguin Books, UK, 1964.

Krippner, Stanley and Rubin, Daniel, eds. *The Kirlian Aura*. Anchor Books, USA, 1974.

Lappé, Frances Moore. *EcoMind*. Nation Books, USA, 2011.

Laszlo, Ervin. *Revolutionary Science – The Rise of the Holistic Paradigm*. 2003.

Litfin, Karen. *Ecovillages – Lessons for Sustainable Community*. Polity Books, USA, 2014.

Lovelock, James. *The Ages of Gaia*. Bantam Books, USA, 1990.

Macnamara, Looby. *People and Permaculture*. Permanent Publications, UK, 2012.

Macy, Joanna. *Despair and Personal Power in the Nuclear Age*. New Society Publishers,USA, 1983.

Maynard, Edward; Thormod, Cathy and Morris, Linda. *Faces of Findhorn*. Findhorn Publications, UK, 1980.

McLaughlin, Corinne with Gordon Davidson. *The Practical Visionary: A New World Guide to Spiritual Growth and Social Change. 2010*. Unity House Publishers, UK, 2010.

Mindell, Arnold. *Sitting in the Fire*. Lao Tse Press, USA, 1995.

Mollison, Bill and Holmgren, David. *Permaculture One*. Tagari, Australia, 1978.

Mollison, Bill. *Permaculture Two*. Tagari, Australia, 1979.

——. *Permaculture – A Designers' Manual*. Tagari, Australia, 1988.

Mollison, Bill and Slay, Reny Mia. *Introduction to Permaculture*. Tagari, Australia, 1991.

Moore, Alanna. *Sensitive Permaculture*. Python Press, Australia, 2009.

Morrow, Rosemary. *Permaculture – Teacher's Notes*. Kangaroo Press, Australia, 1997.

Pearson, David. *The Natural House Book*. Gaia Books, UK, 1989.

——. *Earth to Spirit*. Gaia Books, UK, 1994.

Ray, Paul and Anderson, Sherry. *The Cultural Creatives*. Three Rivers Press, USA, 2000.

Reich, Charles. *The Greening of America*. Penguin, UK, 1970.

Roland, Ethan. *Eight Forms of Capital*. Permaculture Magazine 68, summer 2011.

Roszak, Theodore. *Person/Planet*. Victor Gollancz, UK, 1979.

Sheldrake, Rupert. *The Science Delusion*. Coronet, UK, 2012.

Skinner, Stephen. *Sacred Geometry*. Gaia Books, UK, 2006.

Suchantke, Andreas. *Eco-Geography*. Floris Books, UK, 2001.

Schwenk, Theodor. *Sensitive Chaos*. Rudolf Steiner Press, UK, 1996.

Schwenk, Theodor and Schwenk, Wolfram. *Water – The Element of Life*. Anthroposophic Press, UK, 1989.

Stamets, Paul. *Mycelium Running – How Mushrooms Can Help Save the World*. Ten Speed Press, USA, 2005.

Starhawk. *Truth or Dare: Encounters with Power, Authority and Mystery*. Harper San Francisco, USA, 1988.

Taylor, Gordon Rattray. *How to Avoid the Future*. New English Library, UK, 1977.

Tompkins, Peter and Bird, Christopher. *The Secret Life of Plants*. Allen Lane, UK, 1974.

Wilkes, John. *Flow Forms*. Floris Books, UK, 2003.

Zoeteman, Kees. *Gaia – Sophia, A framework for Ecology*. Floris Books, UK, 1991.

Web References

Ekopia: http://www.ekopia.org.uk/

Findhorn Foundation: http:// www.findhorn.org

Findhorn Press: http:// www.findhornpress.com

Garden Cottage, Graham Bell: http://grahambell.org

Perelandra: http://www.perelandra-ltd.com

Resurgence and Ecologist Magazine: http://www.resurgence.org

Sustainable Yogic Agriculture: http://www.yogicagriculture.org/

Trees for Life: http://www.treesforlife.org.uk

Illustration References

We would like to acknowledge and thank all contributors for the use of their illustrations and photos to this book:

Nina Brun — p. 112.

Roger Doudna — p. 83.

Siobhan Dyson — pp. 52, 72, 74, 87, 102, 121 and 152 (drawings).

Vera Franco — pp. 28, 35, 36, 44, 48 top, 51, 54, 110, 118, 136, 142, 144, 156.

Gilad Margalit — p. 42.

Michael Mitton — pp. 66, 77 bottom, 79, 81 top, 84, 88, 91, 134; front cover photos.

Lyndall Parris — p. 146.

John Talbott — p. 94.

Viljar Valsø — p. 125.

Alan Watson Featherstone — p. 55.

All other illustrations by **Jan Martin Bang**.

About the Authors

JAN MARTIN BANG grew up in England where he was active in the Cooperative and Trade Union Movements in the 1970s. In 1984, he moved to Israel where he was a kibbutz member for 16 years. From 1993 onwards Jan worked on environmental projects within the Kibbutz Movement. This took him on extensive travels within the region, teaching Permaculture courses and visiting ecovillage-type projects in Egypt, Turkey, Cyprus and the Palestinian areas. In 2000, Jan moved with his family to Solborg Camphill Village, where he worked on educational projects with the mentally handicapped, and also with the administration of the Camphill Charitable Trust in Norway. In addition, he edited the Norwegian language magazine, "Landsbyliv" (Village Life), focussing on anthroposophical care work.

Jan has worked with the Global Ecovillage Network since the conference at Findhorn in 1995, first as a contact person in Israel, later as a contributor to the book Ecovillage Living, published in 2002. He has written many articles for commune, community and ecological periodicals over the last two decades, and contributed papers to international conferences on community and ecological issues. In 2004, Jan wrote a section on intentional community in Scandinavia in the four volume Encyclopedia of Community. In 2006, he gained his Diploma in Permaculture from the Nordic Permaculture Institute for his work in education and community building.

Jan has been active in the Norwegian Permaculture movement since 2001, as a member of the Board, and as Chair. He has also been an active member of the Norwegian Ecovillage movement, as Board member and sometime Chair of the Kilden Charitable Trust (inspired by Findhorn!), and currently Jan is the Chair of the Norwegian Ecovillage Association. He has been connected to the International Communal Studies Association since its founding conference in 1985, and in 2010 was elected Chair of the Association.

Jan has written several books about community and environment:
Ecovillages – a practical guide to sustainable communities, 2005.
Growing Eco Communities – practical ways to create sustainability, 2007.
Sakhnin – a portrait of an environmental peace project in Israel, 2009.
The Hidden Seed – the story of the Camphill Bible Evening, 2009.
A Portrait of Camphill, 2010.

CRAIG GIBSONE grew up on a small isolated farm in Australia. Due to being differently able he studied fine arts at the West Australian Institute of Technology before becoming a planetary nomad and ending up in mid-sixties London, where he assisted in creating the "Arts Laboratory", an open space dedicated to exploring the doors of perception.

From there it was a small step in helping to establish the Samyé Ling Monastery and Tibetan Centre in the UK where he immersed himself in an intense three-year period of meditation. Following this he went to live at the Findhorn Community as one of the early pioneers in the emerging communities movement.

Being involved in the Findhorn community for the last 47 years, Craig has been and continues to be an integral part of the development of the community and the ecovillage concept. Previously chair of management for the Findhorn Foundation and trustee, he is the founding director of the pioneering applied ecovillage living course held at the Findhorn Foundation for the past 17 years. Bridging spirituality, shamanism and permaculture, Craig brings a lifetime of practical experience of how to build ecovillages both in the terms of physical, spiritual and social infrastructure necessary for success. As highly experienced and respected elder of the Findhorn Foundation Craig serves currently as Ecovillage Education coordinator at the Findhorn Foundation Ecovillage.

Also of interest from Findhorn Press

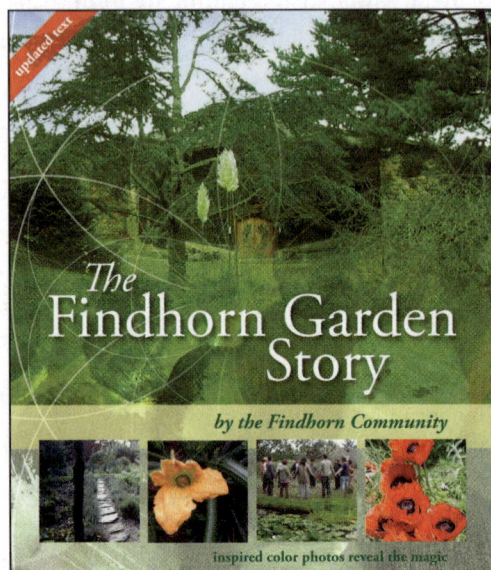

The Findhorn Garden Story
by The Findhorn Community

SHOWCASING WONDERFUL colour photographs, this spiritual classic presents the history and philosophy of Scotland's Findhorn Community. Findhorn was founded more than 40 years ago in far northeast Scotland on windswept and barren sand dunes that happened to sprout a miraculous garden. Plants, flowers, trees, and organic vegetables of enormous sizes began to grow in a small plot around the 30-foot caravan trailer inhabited by three adults and three children living on meager unemployment benefits.

Guidance by God and absolute faith in the art of manifestation led the occupants to this unlikely locale where out of these small beginnings eventually a magical centre emerged that would draw people from all over the world. Their discovery of how to contact and cooperate with the nature spirits and devas that made the garden possible sparked a phenomenon that continues today, as Findhorn has grown into a thriving ecovillage housing hundreds of people from all over the world and an internationally recognized spiritual-learning centre.

978-1-84409-135-5

Also of interest from Findhorn Press

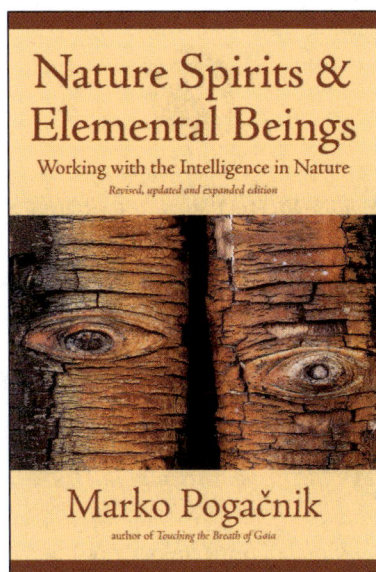

Nature Spirits & Elemental Beings
by Marko Pogacnik

BASED ON FIRSTHAND practical experiences of communicating with natural spirits through meditation, this eye-opening guide to healing the earth teaches how to work with elemental beings, describing each in detail while defining their roles within the web of life.

As a result of tuning in to plants, trees, and animals, and illustrating the disrupted flow of energies within the landscape, the true impact of human culture upon the harmony of the natural world is evocatively revealed.

Insight into related topics, such as how the long-suppressed Goddess culture embraces these energies to make strides toward healing the earth, can set anyone with earth and landscape concerns—gardeners, growers, designers, and builders—one step closer toward becoming environmental warriors.

978-1-84409-175-1

FINDHORN PRESS

Life-Changing Books

Consult our catalogue online
(with secure order facility) on
www.findhornpress.com

For information on the Findhorn Foundation:
www.findhorn.org